Color Plate 1. The black felt peasant vest. Designed and modeled by the author for *Family Circle Fashions and Crafts* © Fall, 1977 and reprinted with their permission.

Color Plate 2. Detail of the black felt vest. Satin stitches of Glosilla thread by Bucilla are the focal point. Cretan stitches hold the shisha mirrors in place.

Color Plate 3. This red sweater was designed by the author for *Family Circle* magazine © January, 1975, and reprinted with their permission. Mirrored flowers also encircle the cuffs.

Color Plate 4. Detail of the flowers with mirrored centers in the red sweater. The flowers are six-strand satin stitches, and French knots dot the flowers.

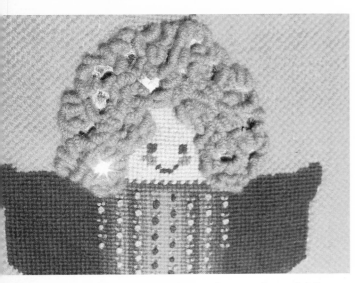

Color Plate 5. Detail of Gwenn Stutzman's angel. Mirrors are held on the needlepoint base with cretan stitching and many bullion stitches. French knots are used for the "roses" on the dress.

Color Plate 6. "Angels We Have Heard On High," a needlepoint pillow designed and stitched by Gwenn Stutzman.

Color Plate 7. "Joy, Joy, Joy," needlepoint pillow designed and worked by Gwenn Stutzman. Several textural stitches were used to add interest. The shisha mirrors add the sparkle!

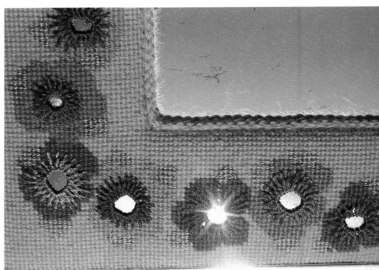

Color Plate 8. Detail of the mirror frame designed by Gwenn Stutzman. The embroidered mirror-centered flowers were added after the needlepoint was completed.

Color Plate 26. Mirrors, ethnic fabric, and "other good things" decorate Diane Powers' charming dolls.

Color Plate 25. "Mother Angel" is one of Diane Power's many mirrored dolls. A tin-framed mirror dots the dolls dress.

Color Plate 28. Three little angels take a stroll on the grass. Shisha mirrors are the stars in their eyes. Designed by Diane Powers.

Color Plate 27. Diane Powers used a mola, tin-framed mirrors, and yarn to make this unusual doll.

Color Plate 29. Marilyn Wein designed this Hostess Apron and Belt for *Woman's Day* magazine. Reprinted with the kind permission of *Woman's Day* magazine. Copyright © 1974 by Fawcett Publications, Inc. See instructions on page 61.

Color Plate 30. Diane Powers used antique mirrored cloth for the wings and the bodice of her "devilish angel" doll.

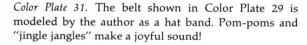

Color Plate 31. The belt shown in Color Plate 29 is modeled by the author as a hat band. Pom-poms and "jingle jangles" make a joyful sound!

Color Plate 32. Diane Powers' "devilish angel" has purple velvet "eye shadow" and stars in her colorful yarn hair. "Shinies" perk up her cheeks.

Shisha Mirror Embroidery

A Contemporary Approach

Jean Simpson

Photographs by Don Rasmussen

Illustrations by Gwenn Stutzman

VNR **VAN NOSTRAND REINHOLD COMPANY**
New York   Cincinnati   Toronto   London   Melbourne

This book is dedicated to my husband, Jim, who has given me the love, encouragement, and freedom to create and to "do my thing," and to our daughters, Jamie, Brooke, and Chelsea, with their flower faces and twinkling eyes. I love you just because you are you.

Photographs by Don Rasmussen, custom prints by Isgo Lepejian, and illustrations by Gwenn Stutzman.

Copyright © 1978 by Litton Educational Publishing, Inc.
Library of Congress Catalog Card Number 78–17836
ISBN 0–442–27641–9

Published in 1978 by Van Nostrand Reinhold Company
A division of Litton Educational Publishing, Inc.
135 West 50th Street, New York, NY 10020, U.S.A.

Van Nostrand Reinhold Limited
1410 Birchmount Road
Scarborough, Ontario M1P 2E7, Canada

Van Nostrand Reinhold Australia Pty. Ltd.
17 Queen Street
Mitcham, Victoria 3132, Australia

Van Nostrand Reinhold Company Limited
Molly Millars Lane
Wokingham, Berkshire, England

16 15 14 13 12 11 10 9 8 7 6 5 4 3 2 1

Library of Congress Cataloging in Publication Data

Simpson, Jean, 1942–
        Shisha mirror embroidery.

        Includes index.
        1. Shisha mirror embroidery. I. Title.
TT778.S55S56   746.4'4   78–17836

ISBN 0–442–27641–9

Contents

Acknowledgments

Without a doubt, this has been the most difficult page to write in the entire book. Words seem so inadequate where people and feelings are involved. I am forever grateful to all of the artists who so generously shared their creations and ideas. Because of you, shisha mirror embroidery will be passed on for future generations to enjoy. To begin with, we have Mumtaz Mahal to thank for her original idea three centuries ago. Thanks to my mother and late father, Dorothy and Ralph Wamser, who deserve both the Parents of the Year Award and the Grandparents of the Year Award *every year!* Thanks to my late grandmother, May West Carpenter, who patiently taught me to embroider when I was three years old. Special thanks to Don Rasmussen, who took all of the beautiful photographs for this book; Gwenn Stutzman, who did all of the exquisite illustrations, as well as many of the creative needlepoint designs; my sister, Debbie Russell, who helped me put my ideas into words; Nora O'Leary, of *Family Circle* magazine, who "discovered" me; Nancy Newman Green and Jean Koefoed of Van Nostrand Reinhold, who were attracted by the glitter of shisha mirrors; Susan Rosenthal of Van Nostrand Reinhold, for her patient and precise editing; and to the following, who have touched my life and my heart in a special way (listed alphabetically); Tony Del Vaglio, Julius Griffin, M. D., Don Scott Holden, M. D., Dr. Norman Vincent Peale, Dr. Frank Richileu, Dr. Robert Schuller, and Annie Williams. Last, but not least, thanks must be given to Mother Nature, whose rainbows and endless beauty are always a source of inspiration to us all.

Introduction

Back in the olden days, before television became a way of life, children used to romp and play in the great outdoors. I didn't. Even though I am a part of the pre-T.V. generation, my activities were limited, due to a bout with rheumatic fever. Instead of romping and playing, I threaded needles and happily stitched away the idle hours. In due time I recovered and I haven't been sick a day since. The only remaining indications of my sedentary youth are fantastically nimble fingers and remarkable lack of coordination in anything remotely athletic!

I managed to graduate from U. C. L. A. (despite my grades in physical education courses) and began teaching elementary school. During the many years that I taught, I took all the art classes that were offered to the teachers. In one of the classes I was introduced to the exciting art of shisha mirror embroidery, which opened up my needlework to totally new horizons. At first, the mirrors were difficult to find; however, undaunted, I substituted pennies and dimes for my "mirror" embroidery. With so many coins stitched onto my clothing, my principal once accused me of looking like a "walking bank."

After "retiring" from teaching several years later to begin my own family, I was asked to teach some needlework classes for adults. By sheer luck, the talent coordinators from the "Dinah Shore Show" wandered into one of my classes. The next thing I knew, I was appearing on national television! That day I received a phone call from a magazine editor. She had seen the show and wanted me to design some mirrored clothing for the magazine.

One outfit led to another, and my "retirement" has kept me two times busier than teaching elementary school ever did. To me, time is *the* most precious commodity. No amount of money can buy extra time. Thus, I try to make each day count. Since all needlework projects require considerable amounts of time, I use the best materials that I can find.

My approach to needlework is like my approach to cooking. I get the general drift of the recipe, but add and subtract ingredients as I go along. Just as I might get an impulse to use cherry pie filling to glaze a ham, so I might add an extra row of stitching around my mirrors. This book has been written for both types of "cooks"—those who like to follow directions to the letter and those who'd rather experiment as they go along. The instructions in Chapter 1 will teach the shisha techniques, and the photographs of finished projects and designs throughout the book will, I hope, serve as inspirations. You will be able to follow my directions exactly or use my designs as springboards to developing your own.

The colors you use in your creations are an intensely personal matter. A color combination that is perceived as pleasing to one person might be hideous to another. There have been volumes upon volumes written on color theory, but I tend to take a very basic approach—if I like the color, I use it! The warm colors (magenta, orange, and vivid yellows) are "my" colors, and I mix them together with great abandon. Don't be afraid to use "your" colors—whatever they may be.

When it comes to design, my approach is best described as "haphazard." I begin with a general idea in mind, but I let the project evolve as I go along. Sometimes the result is like the "Plan Ahead" sign on which there was no room for the "d," and I have to do a lot of ripping out. But, most of the time, a natural and apparently instinctive sense of balance saves me. If you'd rather plan your project before you dive in, then you'll probably follow the given directions exactly and concentrate, perhaps, on perfecting your stitching technique.

Since enjoying life and having fun are important to me, I have tried to make this book enjoyable, as well as informative. I only wish that I could sit and stitch with each one of you personally.

1

Ready, Set, Sew

Shisha mirror embroidery is the ancient East Indian art of stitching bits of mica or mirror to cloth. The Taj Mahal in Agra, India, is not only a world-famous landmark, it is also quite probably the birthplace of shisha mirror embroidery. Shah Jahan built the edifice in honor of his beloved wife, mumtaz Mahal, who has been credited with developing the idea of shisha mirror embroidery circa 1630 A.D. The techniques used today are similar to Mumtaz Mahal's original stitching. If she were alive today, I am certain that Mumtaz Mahal would be delighted that people are still using her technique—one that is over three centuries old.

Shisha mirror embroidery is a deceptively simple needlework technique. You don't need any previous embroidery experience to be successful, and one of the nicest features of shisha mirror embroidery is that you need very little equipment to get started. Embroidery is portable, it can be taken with you to be worked on while you are waiting at appointments or while traveling.

The first questions that you're probably asking yourself are, "What kind of glue do I use?" and "How do I drill holes in the mirrors so that I can sew them on?" The answers are: no glue and no holes! Instead, the mirror is held in place by bringing a thread through the material and making a framework mesh over the mirror. A variety of decorative stitches are then done over the thread framework mesh. And, to anticipate your third question: yes, they can be either washed in the machine or dry-cleaned. Now that that's out of the way, let's get down to the basics.

Mirrors

Shisha means "little glass." Genuine shisha mirrors are made in Pakistan and in India. Since the mirrors are hand-cut, the edges are irregular. However, the irregular edges help to hold the mirrors in the embroidery framework mesh, and are, therefore, an advantage. These edges are completely covered during the process, so you needn't be concerned about their appearance. When the embroidery is complete the framework mesh will have been pulled out toward the edges, leaving just a round area of the mirror in the center. Shisha mirrors are available in the United States in many needlework shops and through mail order (see Suppliers list at the back of the book). Most of the mirrors sold are clear (the traditional type), but some green, blue, or amber ones are available. Red shisha mirrors do exist, but they are extremely rare. Shisha mirrors are washable or dry-cleanable.

Tin-frame mirrors are made in India, and as the name implies, the mirror is encased in a tin frame. They have a cardboard backing and are not washable for that reason. Tin-frame mirrors can be applied in the same manner as you would apply a shisha mirror; that is, by stitching a framework mesh. Other alternatives are to glue them on, or to poke holes in the thin tin edge with an ice pick and then tack them on. A piece of Velcro® can also be attached to the cardboard backing, thus making the mirror both quick to attach and easy to remove. These alternate methods are used when the item onto which these nonwashable mirrors are to be placed requires dry cleaning or washing.

Display mirrors are another alternate mirror type. In the United States display mirrors can be found in floral-supply stores or in hobby shops. Warning! They are neither washable nor dry-cleanable, nor can they be glued on, as their painted backings will come off. They are, therefore, poor candidates for clothing. Also, they are die-cut and their shape is perfectly round. This makes it more difficult to securely anchor them down.

Fabrics, Threads, and Equipment

Any fabric can be decorated with shisha mirrors, as long as it has body. *Cotton, linen, polyester, velvet,* and *wool* are good choices, for example, but chiffon and voile are not suitable. In general, woven fabrics are the easiest ones with which to work, but knits can also be used.

A variety of threads can be used to sew shisha mirrors onto your projects, and you can achieve many special effects and textures just by giving thought to the threads you choose. *Six-strand embroidery floss* is widely available. It can be separated and used in individual strands for a delicate effect, used in six strands as it comes in the skein, or doubled and used as twelve strands for a bolder effect.

D.M.C. pearl cotton is a single-strand thread with a slight twist and sheen. It is made in sizes #1 (very thick), #3 (thick),

#5 (medium), and #8 (fine) and comes in solid colors and variegated skeins. Still another choice is *D.M.C. cotton matte* thread. This is a single-strand thread, and since it is rather thick, it is a good choice for use on muslins or heavier fabrics.

Other than needles and a good pair of *embroidery scissors* tools are not needed. Any good, sharp embroidery or crewel needle with an eye large enough to accommodate your thread is fine. As far as *embroidery hoops* are concerned, some people like to use them and some people don't. I'm one who doesn't. A hoop gets in my way and inhibits my stitching. I feel that if the embroiderer takes care to work with even tension, shisha mirror embroidery can be done without a hoop. If you work more comfortably with a hoop, however, by all means use one. *Thimbles*, too, are a matter of personal choice. If you like them, go ahead and use one.

Shisha Mirror Techniques

There seem to be as many ways to sew on shisha mirrors as there are flavors of ice cream. Read the different methods that follow and then experiment. choose whichever technique is most comfortable and easiest for you.

Regardless of the method you use, remember that the secret of your success is a snugly stitched framework mesh. Just as sturdy houses are built on strong foundations, so it is with shisha mirrors. If your framework mesh is not done correctly, chances are quite good that your mirror will pop out at some point. When making your framework mesh, remember, too, that it is essential to bring the needle up and insert it down *right next to the edge of the mirror.* Also, make certain to pull your stitches firmly.

Two of your immediate questions might be "How do I start?" and "How do I end?" In traditional shisha mirror embroidery, knots are *not* used, a few running stitches hold the thread in place on the reverse side of the material. However, you may either do a few running stitches before you begin or you may knot your thread. The choice is yours. To end the thread, take a few whipstitches on the reverse side of the material.

In the following chapters there are countless photographs of dresses and other items that have been successfully decorated with shisha mirror embroidery. These will, I hope, encourage and inspire you to create your own designs, or, if you wish, copy the designs freehand. But for starters, you might want to transfer some of the design patterns in Chapter 5 or Chapter 2. Be sure to follow the directions for transferring designs to fabric in Chapter 5.

Mumtaz Mahal's Method (see Figure 1–1)
This most traditional method consists of simple cretan stitches. The secret of your success will be a secure framework mesh, so be certain to come up and go down right next to the edge of the mirror.

Figure 1-1. Mumtaz Mahal's Method.

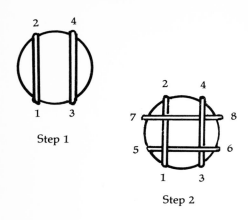

Step 1

Step 2

Bring needle up at 1, down at 2, up at 3, down at 4 (Step 1). Bring needle up at 5, down at 6, up at 7, down at 8. Your framework mesh is now complete (Step 2) and you are ready to begin the stitching around the border of the mirror. As you work, the framework mesh will be covered. Bring needle up at A, and, with the thread counterclockwise and the needle pointing toward you, bring the needle over and then slide it back under the framework mesh, pulling gently toward you (Step 3). With the thread up and the needle pointing toward the left and parallel to the mirror, go down at B and up at C. Pull gently (Step 4). Continue working counterclockwise around the mirror, following the movements in steps 3, and 4 and repeating them over and over until you are all the way around the mirror (Step 5).

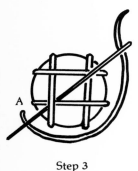

Step 3

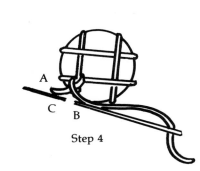

Step 4

Step 5

Result

Figure 1-2. Robert Broyles' Cretan Stitch Method.

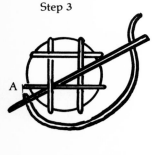

Step 1

Step 2

Robert Broyles' Cretan Stitch Method *(see Figure 1–2)*

The following is Robert Broyles' own version of the cretan stitch method.

Bring the needle up at 1, down at 2, up at 3, down at 4 (Step 1). Bring the needle up at 5, down at 6, (interweaving as in the illustration), up at 7, down at 8. The framework is complete (Step 2). Come up at A and, with the thread counterclockwise and the needle pointing toward you, bring the needle over and slide it back under the framework mesh, pulling gently toward you (Step 3). With the thread to the right and the needle pointing away from you, go down at B and up at C, pulling the needle and thread away from you (Step 4). Continue working counterclockwise around the mirror, following the movements in steps 3 and 4, repeating them all the way around the mirror (Step 5).

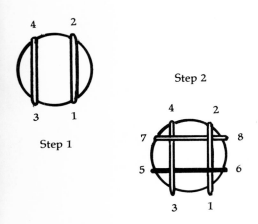

Step 3

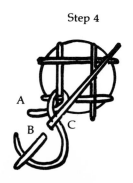

Step 4

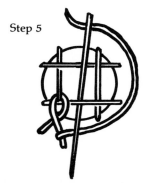

Step 5

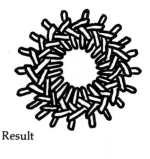

Result

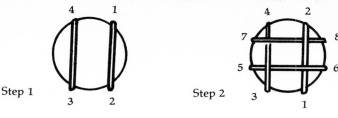

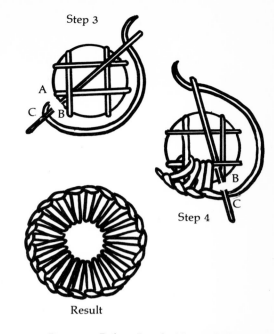

Roberts Broyles' Buttonhole or Blanket Stitch Method (see Figure 1–3)

This method can be used when you want to achieve a plainer, more symmetrical edging around your mirror.

Bring the needle up at 1, down at 2, up at 3, down at 4 (Step 1). Bring the needle up at 5, down at 6, (interweaving as shown in illustration), up at 7, down at 8. Your framework is now complete (Step 2). You are now ready to make the buttonhole or blanket stitch around the mirror. Bring needle up at A. With the thread counterclockwise and the needle pointing toward you, bring the needle over and slide it back under the framework mesh, inserting the needle at B and bringing it up at C. Pull gently (Step 3). Continue working around the mirror counterclockwise, using the movements in Step 4. Be sure to keep the thread counterclockwise and pull the needle over the thread as you pull gently.

Figure 1-3. Robert Broyles' Buttonhole or Blanket Stitch Method.

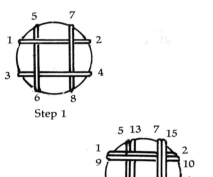

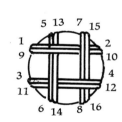

Figure 1-4. Lucy Anderson's Method.

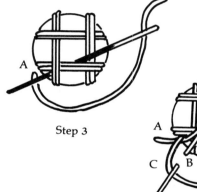

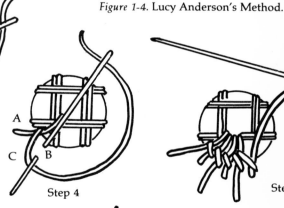

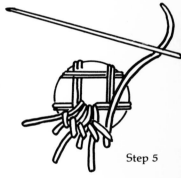

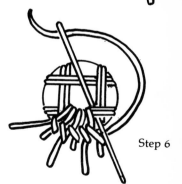

Lucy Anderson's Method (see Figure 1–4)

Lucy Anderson doubles six-strand floss and uses twelve strands to stitch on her mirrors.

Bring the needle up at 1, down at 2, up at 3, down at 4, up at 5, down at 6 (interweaving), up at 7, down at 8 (Step 1). Bring the needle up at 9, down at 10 (either directly on top of 1–2 or directly next to it), up at 11, down at 12, up at 13, down at 14, up at 15, down at 16 (Step 2). Bring the needle up at A. With thread counterclockwise and the needle pointing toward you, bring the needle over and then slide it under the framework mesh and pull gently toward you (Step 3). With the thread counterclockwise and the needle pointing toward you, insert needle at B and come up at C. With the needle over the thread, pull gently toward you (Step 4). Lock the stitch in place by pulling the thread up and to the right (Step 5). Continue working counterclockwise around the mirror by following the movements in steps 3, 4, and 5 (Step 6).

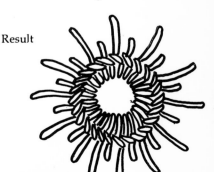

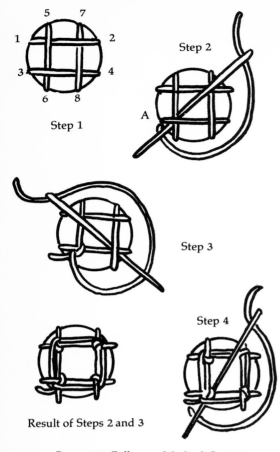

Step 1

Step 2

A

Step 3

Step 4

Result of Steps 2 and 3

Figure 1-5. Folkwear Method © 1976 by Folkwear and reprinted with their permission.

Folkwear Method (see Figure 1–5)

Alexandra Jacopetti of Folkwear Patterns developed an alternate method of attaching the mirrors by securing the thread framework at each intersection.

Bring the needle up at 1, down at 2, up at 3, down at 4, up at 5, down at 6 (interweaving), up at 7, down at 8 (Step 1). Come up at A. With thread counterclockwise and the needle pointing toward you, bring the needle over and then slide it under the cross made by the framework mesh (Step 2). Continue counterclockwise around the mirror, making a knot over the next cross made by the framework mesh (Step 3). There should now be two lines of thread holding the mirror in place. With thread counterclockwise and the needle pointing toward you, bring the needle over and then slide it under the framework mesh. Pull gently (Step 4). With the thread up and the needle pointing toward the left and parallel to the mirror edge, bring the needle down at B and up at C (Step 5). Continue counterclockwise around the mirror.

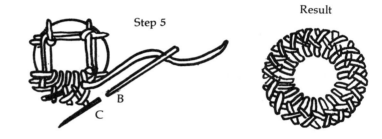

Step 5

Result

Mary Hardy's Lazy Daisy Method (see Figure 1–6)

Mary Hardy has taken the traditional Lazy Daisy stitch and used it to cover the framework mesh. It gives an open airy look.

Bring the needle up at 1, down at 2, up at 3, down at 4. Bring the needle up at 5, and then loop over and under thread 3–4 and 1–2, going down at 6. Bring the needle up at 7, loop over and under thread 3–4 and 1–2, and go down at 8. Bring the needle up at A. With needle pointing away from you, slide the needle under thread 3–4 (Step 1). With thread counterclockwise and needle pointing toward you, bring the needle over and then slide it back under thread 3–4. Go down at B and up at C, pulling needle over the thread and toward you (Step 2). Insert the needle down at D and come up at E (Step 3). Continue working counterclockwise around the mirror, following movements in steps 2 and 3.

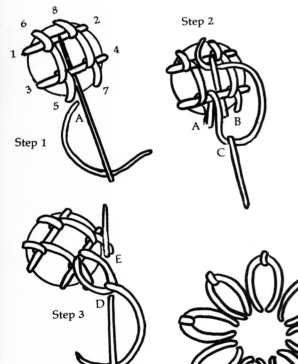

Step 1

Step 2

Step 3

Result

Figure 1-6. Mary Hardy's Lazy Daisy Method.

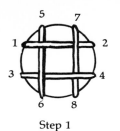

Step 1

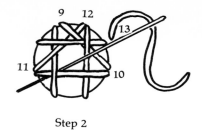

Step 2

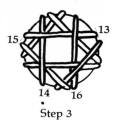

Step 3

Figure 1-7. Alexis Wright's Method.

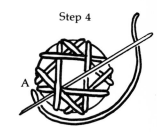

Step 4

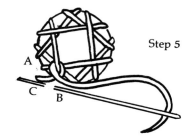

Step 5

Result

Alexis Wright's Method (see Figure 1–7)

Alexis Wright makes her framework mesh by doing several straight stitches over the mirror. The order in which you do the stitches is unimportant. The important thing is to be sure they are snug and that there are enough stitches to hold the mirror in place.

Bring the needle up at 1, down at 2, up at 3, down at 4, up at 5, down at 6 (interweaving), up at 7, down at 8 (Step 1). Bring the needle up at 9, down at 10, up at 11, down at 12, up at 13 (Step 2). Bring the needle down at 14, up at 15, down at 16, (Step 3). The interwoven straight stitches are now in place. Bring the needle up at A. With the thread counterclockwise and the needle pointing toward you, bring the needle over and then slide it under the framework mesh, pulling toward you gently (Step 4). With the thread up and the needle pointing toward the left and parallel to the edge of the mirror, go down at B and up at C (Step 5). Continue working counterclockwise around the mirror, following the movements in steps 4 and 5.

Step 1

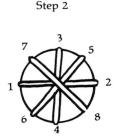

Step 2

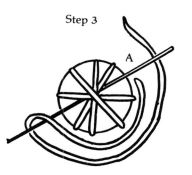

Step 3

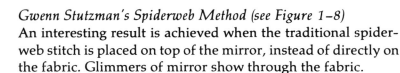

Figure 1-8. Gwenn Stutzman's Spiderweb Method.

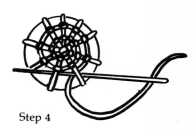

Step 4

Result

Gwenn Stutzman's Spiderweb Method (see Figure 1–8)

An interesting result is achieved when the traditional spiderweb stitch is placed on top of the mirror, instead of directly on the fabric. Glimmers of mirror show through the fabric.

Bring the needle up at 1, down at 2, up at 3, down at 4, up at 5, down at 6 (Step 1). Bring the needle up at 7, down at 8 (Step 2). Bring the needle up at A. Slide the needle under the center intersections and the loop formed by the thread (Step 3). Pull to form a knot. To begin needleweaving slip needle under two spokes, looping around one spoke at a time (Step 4). Continue working clockwise around the spokes.

21

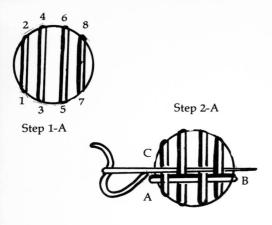

Step 1-A   Step 2-A

Using Four Vertical and Four Horizontal Threads

Gwenn Stutzman's Needleweaving Method (see Figure 1–9)

To achieve an open look a maze of interwoven threads can be used to encase the mirror. No further stitching is necessary. This simple needleweaving technique uses four vertical and four horizontal stitches.

Make the vertical stitches, coming up at 1, down at 2, up at 3, down at 4, up at 5, down at 6, up at 7, down at 8 (Step 1–A). Bring the needle up at A and weave under and over the vertical stitches, going down at B. Bring the needle up at C and weave over and under the vertical stitches (Step 2–A). Continue in this manner.

If you prefer to have three horizontal and three vertical stitches, follow steps 1–B and 2–B.

Result

Figure 1-9. Gwenn Stutzman's Needle-weaving Method.

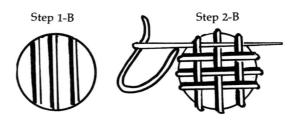

Step 1-B   Step 2-B

Result

Using Three Vertical and Three Horizontal Threads

Figure 1-10. Alexis Wright's Angled Spiderweb Method.

Alexis Wright's Angled Spiderweb Method (see Figure 1–10)

This variation of the spiderweb gives a new slant to mirror embroidery. To achieve the three-dimensional effect a bit of cotton is first placed under the mirror.

Put a bit of cotton under the mirror to set the mirror at an angle (Step 1). Take several straight stitches to hold the mirror in place at the angle (Step 2). Follow the directions for Robert Broyles' Cretan Stitch Method (see Figure 1–2), making some of the "legs" longer than others (Step 3). Continue all the way around the mirror (Step 4). The whipped spiderweb stitch is done over the threads of the legs of the cretan stitches. The stitch is worked clockwise around the mirror. Pass the needle under one leg, looping it up, over, and under the leg, then under the leg to the left. Repeat all the way around the mirror (Step 5). See Figure 1–11 for a look at the finished product.

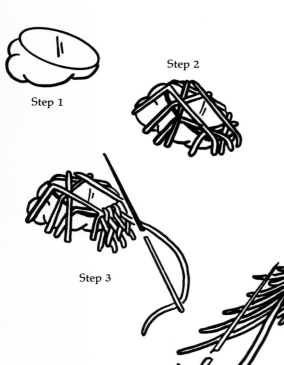

Step 1

Step 2

Step 3

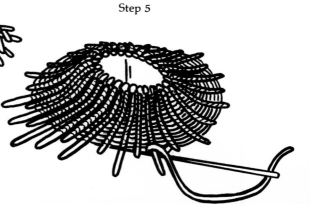

Step 4

Step 5

Figure 2-4. A simple sleeveless zip-front cotton dress became an eye-catcher when Lucy Anderson added mirrors and long and short buttonhole stitches along the neckline and armholes.

Figure 2-5. Sketch of the dress shown in Figure 2-4.

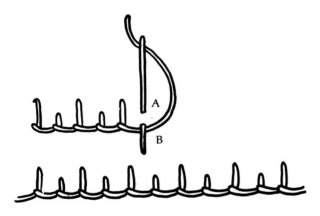

Figure 2-6. Long and Short Buttonhole Stitch. Bring the needle around and down at A and then up at B.

Figure 2-7. Lucy Anderson used spaced, straight satin stitches to cover the seams and add detail to this hot pink and white cotton dress. The mirrors were stitched on with maroon, purple, and cranberry floss. Modeled by the author.

Figure 2-8. Sketch of the dress shown in Figure 2-7.

Figure 2-9. The back of the dress shown in Figure 2-7. Shinies were used as accents.

Figure 2-10. Lucy Anderson added shisha mirrors along the sleeves and shoulders of a simple wool dress. Modeled by Ardys Williams.

Figure 2-11. This muslin shirt provides the background for a sampler of decorative stitches. The shirt is further decorated with machine stitching covering the seams. D. M. C. matte cotton was used to complement the weight of the fabric. Designed by the author and reprinted with the permission of *Ladies Home Journal Needle & Craft* © 1973 by Downe Communications, Inc.

rors for further interest. By the way, this dress is as attractive going as it is coming (see Figure 2-9).

Still another example of what can be done with the basics is the dress shown in Figure 2-10. The sleeves and shoulders are attractively garnished with mirrors. A single ply of mauve-colored Persian yarn was used to attach the mirrors with Lucy Anderson's method (see Figure 1-4). The fluffiness of the wool yarn complements the lush quality of the wool fabric. When working on wool or knit fabrics, remember to keep your stitch tension even and somewhat loose. This allows the fabric and the stitching to "give" as the body moves.

Variations on a Theme

If you are ready to experiment with your stitching, the white muslin blouse sampler shown in Figure 2-11 might be the perfect project for you. After purchasing the blouse, I removed all of the white plastic buttons, dyed them in purple dye, and then sewed them back in place. When you do your dyeing, wear rubber gloves, or else your fingernails will turn purple like mine did! If you don't have a sewing machine that does fancy stitching, try to find a friend who does have one. After all, who wants topstitching lines showing on a beautifully embellished blouse? See Figures 2-12 through 2-19. Scallops, zigzags, and all of the various stitches are possibilities from which to choose. Since the muslin was on the heavy side, D.M.C. article 89, otherwise known as matte cotton,

Figure 2-12. A shisha mirror attached with the buttonhole stitch and surrounded by three more rows of buttonhole stitching.

Figure 2-13. Buttonhole stitching holds the shisha mirror in place, while a row of cretan stitching and French knots surround it.

Figure 2-14. Two rows of buttonhole stitching and French knots surround a shisha mirror.

Figure 2-15. A row of cretan stitching holds the mirror in place and two rows of cretan stitches encircle the mirror.

Figure 2-16. Three rows of cretan stitches and French knots are another way to attach mirrors.

Figure 2-17. A row of cretan stitching holds the mirror, surrounded by two rows of cretan stitches, lazy daisies, straight stitches, and French knots.

Figure 2-18. The mirror is held on with buttonhole stitching and lazy daisies, straight stitches, and French knots complete the circular design.

Figure 2-19. A single row of cretan stitching, surrounded by lazy daisies and straight stitches, holds the mirror down.

Figure 2-20. Vima Micheli wears her teaching sampler blouse. The design was created as she went along; there were no guidelines. For the monochromatic color scheme she used D. M. C. pearl cotton, size # 5, in ecru and beige. The circular stitching around the central mirror was done in knotted detached buttonhole stitches. Modeled by the designer.

Figure 2-21. Detail of the blouse shown in Figure 2-20. Vima Micheli, the designer, concentrates her stitching on one area of the garment and relies on the texture of many stitches for surface interest.

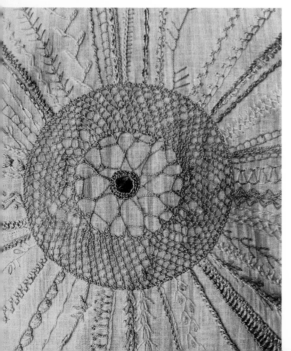

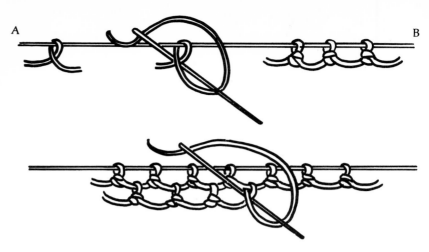

Figure 2-22. Vima Micheli's knotted detached buttonhole method. Working from left to right, bring the needle up at A and down at B.

seemed like the perfect thread to use. Matte cotton is single strand so it won't separate, and it has a sturdy look. I used approximately one skein each in the following rainbow-bright colors: red, orange, yellow, parrot green, turquoise, purple, and hot pink. Add or subtract colors as you wish, but use a total of seven to eight skeins. A good rule of thumb is the thicker the thread you use, the more of it you will need to complete a project.

The designer of the blouse in Figure 2–20 doesn't draw guidelines on her projects, as she finds them inhibiting. She likes to do a mass of stitching in one area of the garment so that the various areas don't have to compete for the eye's attention. The blouse shown is crushed gauze and has expansive work on the back in shades of ecru and beige. The center mirror is surrounded by her "Knotted Detached Buttonhole" and the various lines of stitching radiate out from the center like spokes of a wheel (see Figure 2–21). Figure 2–22 will show you the knotted detached buttonhole. The spokes were done in chains (twisted, cabled, and square), herringbones, wrapped herringbones, wrapped and whipped back stitches, Pekinese stitches, Portuguese stem stitches, palestrinas and French knots (see *The Stitches of Creative Embroidery*, by Jacqueline Enthoven, Van Nostrand Reinhold, © 1964). Different textures and reliefs were achieved by using D.M.C. pearl cotton in sizes #3, and #5, embroidery floss, D.M.C. matte cotton (article 89), linen, French silk, and wool. D.M.C. pearl cotton, size #1, was used for couching only, as it is too thick to be pulled through the fabric. Approximately two skeins of each type of thread were used in shades of ecru, cream, beige, eggshell, bone, and white. It is important that to be able to wash the finished garment, you must use washable threads in your stitching. Because wool and silk were used, this sampler blouse must be dry-cleaned.

In Figure 2–23 the same designer again used her detached knotted buttonhole technique, only this time on a sleeve of a blue cotton tunic. In this instance, a single mirror was used. A tassel adds movement to the design. On the front center neckline of the tunic she sewed several mirrors in a normal fashion and then connected them with the detached knotted buttonhole (see Figure 2–24). She used approximately four skeins of French blue D.M.C. pearl cotton, size #5, for the stitching and tassels on this blue-on-blue design.

A perfect way to give emphasis to mirrors is to use needleweaving. Needleweaving is a technique combining elements of embroidery and weaving. An odd number of warp threads are secured to the fabric (attached at the beginning and end, but left loose in between). A second thread is used to weave over and under the warp threads. (See *Needle Lace and Needleweaving*, by Jill Nordfors, Van Nostrand Reinhold,© 1974.) The sleeves of a rather plain orange cotton dress struck one designer as a perfect spot to make a flower garden (see Figure 2–25 showing detail of the sleeve). To do the needleweaving follow the directions in Figure 2–26. The designer suggests that you attach the warp threads snugly, using D.M.C. pearl cotton, size #5. Making sure the warp threads are not pulled together or otherwise distorted, thread D.M.C. pearl cotton, size #3, into a blunt tapestry needle and weave over and under the warp threads. Do this weaving in a relaxed, but not loose, manner so that every thread is visible and the ridges that form can be noticed. Approximately four skeins of D.M.C. pearl cotton, size #3, and one skein of D.M.C. pearl cotton, size #5, were used for the perky orange flowers. French knots in D.M.C. pearl cotton, size #3, complete the effect.

Figure 2-23. An elaborate version of the knotted detached buttonhole method was used by Vima Micheli for the sleeve of a blue blouse. A tassel adds motion to the design.

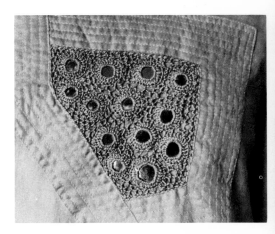

Figure 2-24. Vima Micheli connected her mirrors with detached knotted buttonhole stitches. The color scheme of this soft cotton tunic is blue-on-blue.

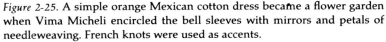

Figure 2-25. A simple orange Mexican cotton dress became a flower garden when Vima Micheli encircled the bell sleeves with mirrors and petals of needleweaving. French knots were used as accents.

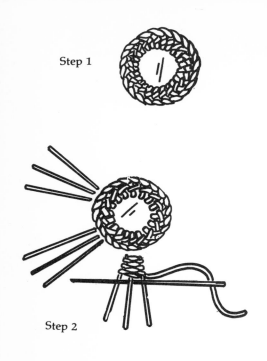

Step 1

Step 2

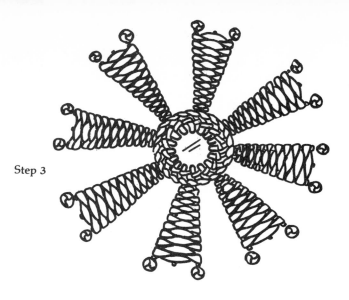

Step 3

Figure 2-26. Vima Micheli's method of needleweaving. Attach the mirror. Using D. M. C. Pearl Cotton, size # 5, make three lines. Using D. M. C. pearl cotton, size # 3, and a blunt tapestry needle, make three straight lines. Weave over and under. Shisha mirror is attached in a normal fashion before you begin the needleweaving. The dots are the French knots.

Figure 2-27. A cotton T-shirt was taken out of the ordinary with grosgrain ribbons and mirrors. Designed by the author and reprinted with the permission of *Family Circle* magazine © February, 1975.

Mirrors with Embellishments

Shisha mirrors are dazzling all by themselves, but can become even more spectacular when ribbons, beads, bells, or lace are added. The results can be unique and dramatic!

Ribbons

Ribbons are available in a wide range of widths and textures—satin, grosgrain, picot-edged, patterned, plaid, polka dot, and so forth. Adding a bit of ribbon can turn a plain-Jane outfit into a showstopper. Before you sew ribbons onto your garment, test them for washability and preshrink them if necessary. It's better to spend the few minutes it takes ahead of time than to have a puckery mess later!

To make the ribboned T-shirt shown in Figure 2–27, I used six different colors and three different widths of washable grosgrain ribbons—1 yard each of ½-inch bright green and turquoise, ¾-inch orange and magenta, and 1-inch turquoise and light orange. One skein of embroidery floss in each of the ribbon colors was more than enough to attach the mirrors using Robert Broyles' cretan stitch method (see Figure 1–2). Profit by mistake! I originally placed the T-shirt on a flat surface and laid the ribbons on it in a pleasing geometric pattern. I then used Stitch Witchery®, a fusible webbing that is available at most notion counters, and cut tiny strips the same widths as the ribbons. With a hot iron, I pressed the ribbons on. To appreciate the full effect of my new top I decided to try it on. To my horror the ribbons popped off! So, the solution is to put the T-shirt on first and *then* pin the ribbons on it. (T-shirts give and ribbons don't.) When you have the ribbons pinned in just the right spots use either Stitch Witchery® and a hot iron or stitch the edges of the ribbon on the sewing ma-

Figure 2-28. Grosgrain ribbons were stitched onto a beach coverup in a harlequin design. Occasional mirrors dot the diamond shapes. Designed by the author and reprinted with the kind permission of *Family Circle* magazine © July, 1975.

Figure 2-29. This dress sleeve features herringbone stitching over grosgrain ribbons. Designed by Lucy Anderson.

chine. If you do decide to stitch the ribbons by machine and you don't want to change thread and bobbin for each color, try using the clear nylon thread.

Another example of ribbon with shisha mirror embroidery is shown in Figure 2–28. Here brightly colored 1-inch grosgrain ribbons form a harlequin design on the white beach coverup. The whole coverup is washable. A mirror dots the center of each diamond shape. For the ties, a two-toned bow effect was achieved by using one color of ribbon on one side and another color ribbon on the other side. A total of 15 yards of 1-inch wide grosgrain ribbon was needed to make this coverup. I used 3 yards of magenta, tangerine, parrot green, peacock blue, and lemon yellow. A total of 2½ yards of ¼-inch grosgrain ribbon was needed for the two-toned ties—½ yard each of the colors listed above. Approximately two skeins each of magenta, tangerine, parrot green, peacock blue, and lemon yellow embroidery floss were used to do the mirror embroidery.

Actually, the possibilities for shisha mirror embroidery and ribbon combinations are endless. Figure 2–29 shows grosgrain ribbon given a new look with herringbone stitching and some shisha mirrors. A shadow effect can be achieved by using one color of ribbon and a different color of pearl cotton for the stitching on top of it. Figures 2–30-A and 2–30-B show how to make the herringbone stitch over ribbon. Still another possibility is to tack down narrow widths of ribbon with straight stitches. Butt the edges of ribbon together to make broad bands of color (see Figure 2–31). Vary the shades from dark to light or try for a rainbow effect.

Herringbone Stitch Over Grosgrain Ribbon

Figure 2-30. Herringbone stitch and herringbone stitches over grosgrain ribbon. Bring the needle up at 1, down at 2, up at 3, down at 4, and so on.

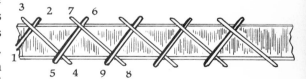

Herringbone Stitch over Grosgrain Ribbon

Figure 2-31. Margot Blair tacks down several narrow grosgrain ribbons in a rainbow of colors, from dark to light, by making straight stitches over them.

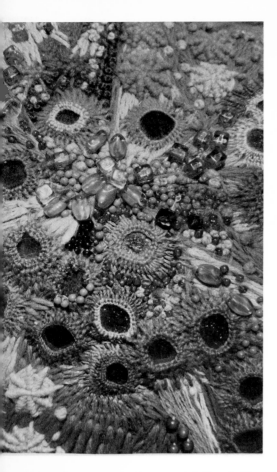

Figure 2-32. A crusty, Medieval effect was achieved by Esther Feldman when she used colored shisha mirrors and lavishly embellished them with beads.

Beads

Beads come in wood, plastic, glass, and metal. Sprinkled here or there or in great clusters, they can add lots of pizazz to your clothing. Test to be sure that the beads are washable or dry-cleanable. (Some plastic beads dissolve in dry-cleaning fluid.) Figure 2–32 shows a variety of beads mixed together with shisha mirrors for an elaborate effect. Here too you are limited only by your imagination.

Beads can be sewn on using regular thread (doubled to make it stronger), embroidery thread, nylon thread, or dental floss. The first step is to cut a piece of thread approximately 2 feet long and knot the end. Come up from the underside of the fabric and pull the needle and thread until the knot is secure under the fabric. Slip the needle through the holes in the bead, insert the needle into the fabric, and pull the thread down to the underside of the fabric. Bring the needle and thread up in the next spot and repeat. Continue until the thread is used up. As you end your work, make a few whipstitches on the underside of the fabric and clip the tail.

To add dangling rows of beads pull the knotted thread until the knot is secure under the fabric and then string as many beads as desired onto the needle and thread. After the last bead has been strung, reverse the direction of the needle and insert the needle into the next to the last bead. Thread back through the row of beads and insert your needle into the fabric near where you came up. Tack on the underside with a few whipstitches and cut the thread. There will be thread showing on the outside of the last bead in the row, but this will be less noticeable if you use a smaller bead at the end. Each dangling row of beads should be done with a new thread.

Bells

Lots of mothers tie bells to their toddler's shoelaces; the children love the sound and the bells serve a purely practical purpose should a child wander off in the supermarket. Adults can enjoy the same sound by sewing bells to their clothing. Tiny Pakistani "dancing bells" can be found at many import stores, as well as those listed in the Suppliers list at the back of this book. If you tend to talk a great deal with your hands, you'd better refrain from sewing large numbers of bells on your sleeves, lest you drown out your own words! On the other hand, bells on the skirt of a long evening dress can make delightful sounds when you are dancing. I personally like tiny bells sewn on my everyday dresses.

Shinies

"Shinies" are tiny, medium, or large discs, coins, teardrops, or any piece of metal that reflects the light. Tiny holes or loops make sewing easier. If your shinies don't have loops or holes, find someone with a tiny drill bit and let them buzz away! Brass or copper sheeting can be purchased in hobby shops, cut into shapes, and a tiny hole can be punched with an ice pick. Presto! You have homemade shinies. If you'd rather purchase shinies, see the Suppliers list in the back of the book.

Figure 2-33. A variety of needlework techniques were used to enhance the neckline of this sleeveless dress. Appliquèd shapes, mirrors, beads, and bells were added. Designed by Lucy Anderson.

Figure 2-33 shows how a combination of beads, bells, and shinies livened up a sleeveless dress. Petal shapes of pink and mauve pin-striped cotton fabric were appliquéd onto a purple cotton dress. Burgundy-colored embroidery floss was used for the cretan stitching that surrounds the petal shapes. The shisha mirrors were attached using Lucy Anderson's method (see Figure 1-4) in rust, wine, plum, and rose embroidery floss. A total of six skeins was used. The tiny "dancing bells" were added last.

The yellow and orange sun halter in Figure 2-34 was made for me. I added amber mirrors and shinies to give it a warm sunshine glow. One skein each of D.M.C. pearl cotton, size #5, in orange, burnt orange, and golden yellow, was used for the cretan stitching around the mirrors. The amber mirrors were added randomly in a sunburst pattern.

Lace

The old-world charm of lace, accented with mirrors, makes for striking results. Lace can be found stashed away in attics, and trunks, or, if you aren't fortunate enough to have relatives who save bits and pieces of nostalgia, you can visit your local thrift shop. Old tablecloths, collars, cuffs from dresses of yesteryear, and the doilies that Granny used on the arms of her chairs can all be put to good use.

An aged, square, lace and linen tablecloth was the inspiration for the lovely summer evening poncho shown in Figure 2-35. The entire linen center was removed from the cloth and the remaining lace border was handstitched onto an ecru Ultrasuede® poncho. Approximately eight skeins of embroidery floss were used for the buttonhole stitching that attached the lace to the poncho. Mirrors were embroidered with twelve strands of ecru floss, using Lucy Anderson's method (see Figure 1–4). The circular mirror design repeats

Figure 2-34. Amber shisha mirrors and gold "shinies" decorate the sun-printed fabric of this halter. Designed by Lucy Anderson and the author. Modeled by Ardys Williams.

Figure 2-35. An old lace tablecloth was transformed by Lucy Anderson into an elegant evening poncho. The stitching around the mirrors subtly accents the rounded motif of the lace.

Figure 2-36. Detail of the lace-and-mirror poncho shown in Figure 2-35.

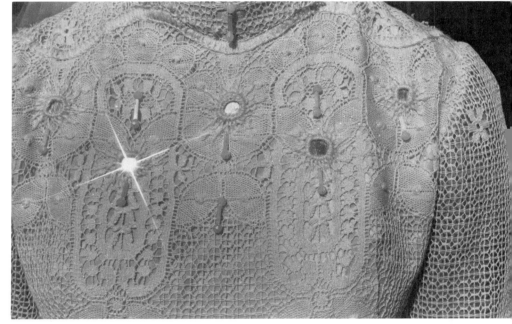

Figure 2-37. Lucy Anderson made this elegant wedding dress for her future daughter-in-law, Cheryl.

Figure 2-38. The crown and veil for the wedding dress shown in Figure 2-37.

Figure 2-48. Lucy Anderson's nimble fingers turned this simple sewing pattern into a spectacular dress with insets of ethnic fabrics and mirrors.

Figure 2-49. The back of the dress shown in Figure 2-48 is just as pretty as the front.

Figure 2-50. A potpourri of stitching techniques were used to accent the sleeves of a Guatemalan dress. Designed by Nan Ferrin.

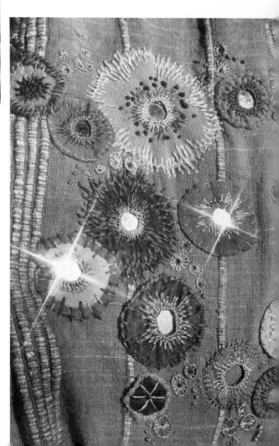

Figure 2-51. An antique mirrored cloth band was placed around the bodice of this dress. Designed and modeled by Lucy Anderson.

Figure 2-53. The past was improved upon when cretan stitches, French knots, and buttonhole stitches in brightly colored pearl cotton were added to this antique piece. Designed by Margo Blair.

Figure 2-52. Margo Blair mixed the past and the present in her mauve and purple top. Printed fabrics were pieced together and inset with a piece of antique mirrored fabric.

Figure 2-51). Another designer combined antique mirror cloth with present-day fabric in a blouse (see Figures 2-52 and 2-53). After inserting a remnant of mirror cloth into her multi-print cotton blouse, the designer re-embroidered the antique mirror cloth (see Figure 2-53). She used cretan, buttonhole, and French knots in D.M.C. pearl cotton, size #5. This blouse is a perfect example of combining the old and the new.

Iron-on Transfer Designs

Commercially made iron-on transfers are actually outlines of designs, often on tissuelike paper. The sheet of paper is inverted and, with a hot, dry iron, the design is transferred onto your own piece of fabric. Just as children like the security of following lines in a coloring book, many stitchers (I am one of them) are lovers of iron-on transfer designs. Many pattern companies have jumped on the bandwagon and now offer a variety of embroidery transfer designs. There are several ways to proceed if you wish to make your own transfer designs or use the designs I've given in this chapter. Hectograph pencils (see Suppliers list at the back of the book and exact instructions for use of hectograph pencils in Chapter 5) and a hot iron work beautifully. Another choice is to use dressmaker's carbon (see instructions for the black felt vest on page 46). In either case, all you have to do is to decide where to place the design, transfer it, and start stitching.

When you are using an iron-on transfer design, don't worry about the lines showing outside your embroidery. Dry cleaning or washing will usually make them disappear.

To begin with, Figure 2-54 and Color Plate 4 show a sweater that I decorated by placing a floral motif around the neckline. To avoid stretching the knit as I worked, I basted a layer of net around the neckline on the inside of the sweater. I satin-stitched the garland of flowers onto the red knit sweater, using embroidery floss in goldenrod, magenta, hot pink, and purple. The French knots were made using the leftover thread, and they were done after the satin stitching. The leaves were of emerald green and pine green Glosilla® by Bucilla (see Supplier's list at the back of the book.) Approximately two skeins of each green shade were needed. After the flower embroidery was complete, I cut away the net with cuticle scissors. This technique should be followed for just about all embroidery on knit fabrics. The same flower transfer designs (see instructions in Figure 2-55) were used on a hot pink and orange Indian cotton outfit. After ironing on the transfers, a mirror was placed in the center of each flower, using the cretan stitch method (see Figure 1-2). Next, the satin stitching was done with six-strand embroidery floss. French knots were again added last and provided textural accent. The leaves, done in the fishbone stitch, were also stitched in six-strand embroidery floss. Each flower took approximately one skein of D.M.C. embroidery floss. The colors used were tangerine,

Figure 2-54. Shiny mirrors and silky flowers adorn the neckline of this red knit sweater. Designed by the author for *Family Circle* magazine. January, 1975 and reprinted with their permission.

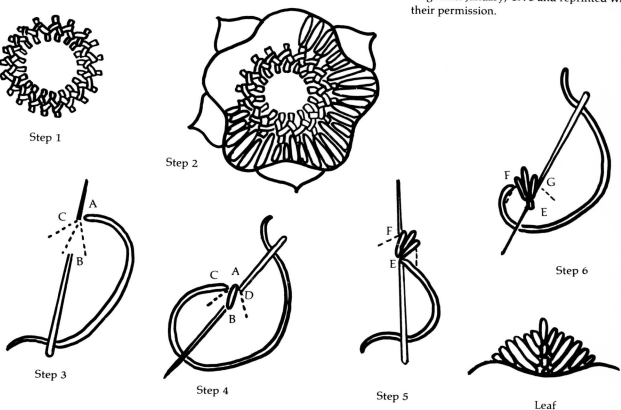

Figure 2-55. The flower shape transfer design used in Figure 2-54 and 2-56.

Figure 2-56. Here the flower shapes were used to enhance a jacket. The necklace was made from pom-poms, and "jingle jangles" from India. Designed by the author for *Family Circle* magazine © May, 1977 and reprinted with their permission.

orange, yellow, goldenrod, purple, and plum. Two skeins each of emerald green and chartreuse floss were used for the leaves. The finished product is shown in Figure 2-56.

I learned an important lesson while making the black felt vest shown in Color Plate 1: wool felt shrinks if steamed! I had spent several days doing the satin stitching on the vest and was so pleased with my efforts that I decided to steam the piece. Before my eyes, it shrank up to one-half its original size. I had to start all over! Since it is difficult to trace a design onto black felt, I traced the shapes (see Figure 2-57) onto paper, laid white dressmaker's carbon on the felt, carbon side down, and placed the pattern on top of the two layers. With a paper clip that I had opened, I poked all around the design lines every 1/8 inch or so. This resulted in a dotted line on the black felt. I then used fabric paint in a ball-point tube to trace around the design so I could see the lines clearly (see Color Plate 1 for the finished vest).

Mirrors for Men

The fashion pendulum has once again swung to the position where men's clothes are colorful and expressive of their particular life-styles. Frilly tuxedo shirts, heavily embroidered casual shirts, and studded blue jeans are all signs of the times. Five years ago, the only mirrored men's shirts or slacks I designed were for entertainers (see Figures 2-58 and 2-59). The hems of these slacks were adorned with amber mirrors, sewn on using the cretan stitch method (see Figure 1-2). Two skeins each of D.M.C. pearl cotton, size #3, in ecru, goldenrod, sienna, and rust were used to attach the mirrors. Feather stitching, done in gold metallic thread, was interspersed among the mirrors, and the stitching ties the V-shaped symmetrical design together. Metallic threads should be used in short lengths, as they tend to fray when they are pulled through fabric.

Nowadays, mirrors on men's everyday sport clothes are becoming more of an everyday sight. For example, the handsome shirt in Figure 2-60 is attractive, yet in no way feminine. Using the lazy daisy method of stitching on the mirrors (see Figure 1-6) the designer worked with pearl cotton in size #5 to make cascades of flowers around the armhole, collar, and cuffs. The mirrors were randomly attached, using one skein of lemon D.M.C. pearl cotton, size #3, and one skein each of D.M.C. pearl cotton, size #5, in orange, tangerine, and peach. French knots were clustered around each mirror in the remaining threads. One skein of D.M.C. pearl cotton, size #3, in bright green was used to embroider the leaves that meander in flowing lines through the flowers. As a final touch, lazy daisy stitches were added around each buttonhole.

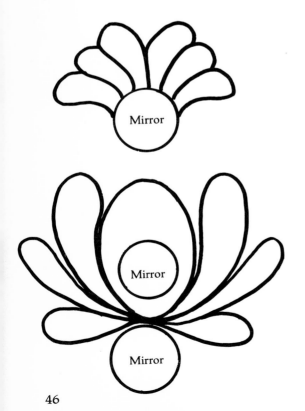

Figure 2-57. The shapes used for the black vest shown in Color Plate 1.

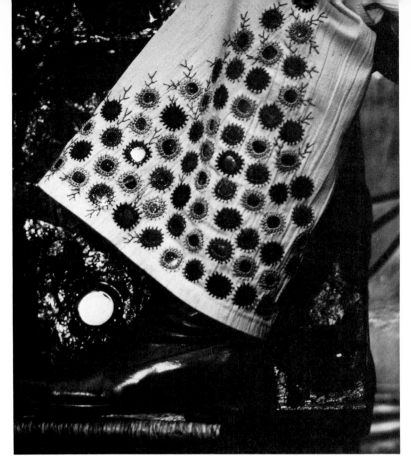

Figure 2-58. These slacks were made for composer and entertainer, Lee Dresser, as a gift. Metallic thread and D. M. C. pearl cotton, size # 3, were used to hold the amber mirrors in place on the crushed muslin pants. Feather stitching was used as accent between the mirrors. Designed by the author.

Figure 2-59. The outfit shown in Figure 2-58. Mirrors on the shirt collar, placket, and cuffs reflect the spotlight shining on the singer.

Figure 2-60. Garlands of colorful flowers, all done in the lazy daisy stitch, were embroidered in pearl cotton on this blue denim workshirt. Designed by Mary Hardy for her son.

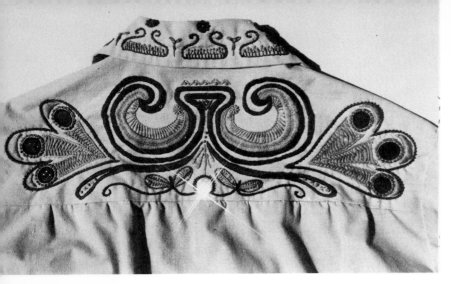

Figure 2-61. Alexis Wright proved that mirror embroidery can be "masculine" with this shirt that she made for her husband, Chester. The front and back yokes, as well as the cuffs, are all heavily stitched. Alexis believes that embroidery should be washable and last forever, so she used heavy Mexican cotton fabric in turquoise.

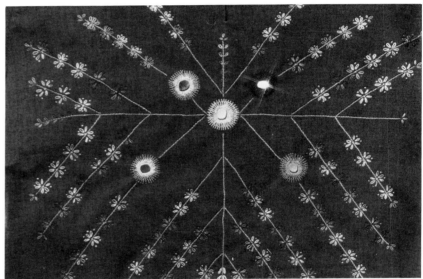

Figure 2-62. A Mexican tablecloth design inspired Sylvia Campbell to make this colorful shirt for her husband. The flowers were embroidered in variegated pearl cotton, and the fabric is a rich chocolate-brown kettle cloth, washable, of course!

Figure 2-63. The shirt shown in *Figure 2-62.* The typical Mexican styling suits the Mexican-inspired embroidery.

Figure 2-61 shows a cotton shirt with embroidered yoke and cuffs. The design and texture of the stitching is heavy and masculine. The stitches used were chains, detached lazy daisies, lazy daisies, spiderwebs, buttonholes, satins, stems, van dykes, cretans, French knots, and long-legged French knots. Two skeins of D.M.C. embroidery floss in each of the following colors were used: wine red, old gold, deep avocado green, light avocado green, lavender, periwinkle blue, and dark green. Amber shisha mirrors were sewn onto the design using Alexis Wright's method (see Figure 1-7). It's a perfect example of current ways of using embroidery in men's fashions, as is the shirt shown in Figures 2-62 and 2-63. A Mexican tablecloth served as an inspiration for this shirt. One skein of variegated D.M.C. pearl cotton, size #5, in shades of pink, and one skein in shades of yellow, was used for the lazy daisy stitch, which formed the flowers, as well as for the French knots surrounding them. The stems were done in the stem stitch, using one skein of variegated D.M.C. pearl cotton, size #5, in shades of green. The mirrors were attached with closely spaced cretan stitches (see Figure 1-2). The shirt itself was made from chocolate brown kettle cloth.

Figure 2-64. A single row of cretan stitching holds each mirror in place on this denim shirt, and feather stitching gives it a finished look. All the embroidery was done in pearl cotton, size # 3. Designed by the author and modeled by her husband, Jim.

Figure 2-65. Gwenn Stutzman designed this sturdy denim workshirt embroidered with a seagull, vines, and flowers stitched in D. M. C. pearl cotton. Modeled by Don Rasmussen.

Figure 2-66. Detail of the shirt shown in Figure 2-65. Note the spiderweb method of attaching the shisha mirror on the pocket. Snaps make the shirt easy to get on and off.

With the addition of shisha mirrors, cretan stitches, and feather stitches, the collar, cuffs, and front placket became the focal point of the shirt shown in Figure 2-64. This inexpensive permanent press workshirt was spruced up with one skein each of yellow, orange, purple, magenta, and green D.M.C. pearl cotton, size #3. The feather stitching was done in green and was used to tie the design together. The decoration is simple, but effective. More elaborate decoration was done on the shirt shown in Figures 2-65 and 2-66. A seagull flies over the heart, and mirrors, flowers, and vines are scattered on the front and back yoke. The designer used D.M.C. pearl cotton, sizes #3 and #5, in dark, medium, and light yellow, and in orange, light blue, red, green, and white. The seagull was done in satin and stem stitching. The mirrors were attached using the cretan stitch method (see Figure 1-2), with the exception of one mirror on the front pocket flap that was attached using the spiderweb method (see Figure 1-8). Other stitches that the designer used are the fly, lazy daisy, French knot and double cross.

Men's shirts and pants are not the only items that can be enhanced with the addition of mirrors. Here are just a few ideas to start your creative wheels whirring: mirrored tennis racket covers, tennis hats, and warm-up jackets and pants. Mirrors on neckties, on fabric or needlepointed belts, and on cummerbunds are also possibilities. What about mirrors on vests or on golf club covers? The list can go on and on.

Mirrors for Children

Kids' clothing should be both indestructible and adorable. The clothes have to withstand mud pies, poster paint, and misplaced bubble gum (if it doesn't land in the child's hair first). You must be able to toss children's garments into the washer and dryer and miraculously have them come out looking like new. If you're wondering about the washability of mirrored embroidered garments, the answer is, yes. They are washable and very durable, and mirrors can be used to cover a multitude of "accidents" (grease spots, grass stains, mustard dribbled from a luscious hot dog, and the all-time favorite, chocolate fudge stains). Remember to use sturdy fabrics if the mirrored item will be used for rough playing. It seems a shame to spend time mirroring inexpensive cloth that will tear or rip after the first few wearings. By the way, I've never met a child who doesn't love little extras on his or her clothes—pockets, appliqués, buttons—and shisha mirrors make perfect extras.

Mirrors have proven to be a utilitarian, as well as a decorative, addition to my own children's clothing. When my youngest daughter first discovered scissors, her favorite pastime was to snip holes in anything and everything that didn't move. The day I found her brand-new pants filled with neatly snipped, pea-sized holes could have been a whole (no pun intended) lot worse had it not been for shisha mirror embroidery. I simply covered over each hole with a shisha mirror. In Figure 2-67 these pants are modeled by a little neighbor who is their current owner. They are still wearable three years later. Both little girls in the photograph are wearing terry cloth beach robes that were originally made for my little girls. This proves the durability of mirrors and their ability to withstand repeated washings. The shisha mirrors were attached using D.M.C. pearl cotton.

The dress in Figure 2-68 has several rows of delicate cretan stitching in D.M.C. pearl cotton, size #5, encircling each mirror (see Figure 2-69). Approximately one skein each of peacock blue, yellow, hot pink, and orange were used for the embroidery. The repetition of the circles and the simplicity of the overall design enhance the dress without overpowering the wearer. Happy news! The dress is made of crushed muslin and the whole thing, mirrors and all, is washable.

Figure 2-67. A single row of stitching holds the mirrors on these terry cloth beach outfits, and feather stitching provides an airy look and continuity. Designed by the author. Modeled by Suzie and Juliana Holmstrom.

Figure 2-68. This dress of crushed muslin is completely washable, mirrors and all. Designed by Geri Haname. Modeled by the author's daughter, Brooke.

Figure 2-69. Detail of the dress shown in Figure 2-68. Delicate cretan stitches in D. M. C. pearl cotton, size # 5, encircle the mirrors.

Children love hats. After I completed a white felt beret, my daughter took it for her own (see Figure 2-70). A single row of cretan stitching holds the mirrors in place, and feather stitching gives an overall continuity to the mirrored beret.

Children love festive clothing, too. An antique choli is pictured in Figure 2-71. Notice the tiny chain stitches and mirrors that embellish the choli.

Besides covering up holes, a combination of appliqué, embroidery, and mirrors can be the perfect solution for covering up impossible-to-remove stains. (Why do they always seem to appear most often on brand-new clothing?) Other ideas for using the mirrors for children's things are: on dirty-clothes bags, on sleeping bag covers, on tennis racket covers, and on sweaters, T-shirts, and tops of all kinds. A mirrored rainbow on a pant leg or a row of mirrors covering up the crease of a let-down hem are other ideas.

Figure 2-70. This mirrored beret incorporates cretan and feather stitching. Designed by the author for *Family Circle* magazine © February, 1975 and reprinted with their permission. Modeled by the author's daughter, Chelsea.

Figure 2-71. This antique choli, from India, is part of the author's collection. Modeled by the author's daughter, Jamie Lynn.

52

3

Accents and Accessories

An understated dress on Sunday can become a conversation piece at dinner on Monday with the additions of accents and accessories! Or, if you circle your waist with a glistening belt or slip on a pair of mirrored shoes, your friends won't notice that you have on that same old dress again! It's fun to make a fashion statement with accessories. So, if everything in your closet has the blahs, shine them up with shishas!

Neckwear

We'll start off with the *chatelaine* shown in Figure 3-1. *Chatelaine* is a French word meaning "keeper of the keys." Chatelaines were traditionally made from silver and were often inset with jewels. Women wore chatelaines either around their necks or waists, and they were used to hold household essentials—bobbins, pencils, needles, crochet hooks, and tape measures. Figures 3-1 and 3-2 show precisely what this modern version of a chatelaine looks like. The designer uses it to hold scissors, needles, and other embroidery supplies. It was constructed using a small (about 5- by 5-inch) piece of #13 mono needlepoint canvas. Approximately twenty yards of Persian wool yarn were used for the background covering on the canvas, which was done in a variety of stitching techniques. The top module (see Figure 3-2) has a mirror in the center surrounded by tightly packed bullion stitches (see Figure 3-3). D.M.C. pearl cotton, size #3, in a variety of colors was used for the bullion stitches. The tassels were made from various colors of six-strand embroidery floss. There is a pocket on the back to hold tissues, etc. The two lower modules, which also have pockets on the back to hold tiny scissors or needles, can be unscrewed to allow the top module to be worn as a piece of jewelry around the neck.

Figure 3-1. The chatelaine designed by Vima Micheli. Canvas was covered in black wool, and a variety of colors formed the packed bullion stitches around the mirror. The tassles were made from embroidery floss.

Figure 3-2. Detail of the packed bullion stitches shown in Figure 3-1.

Figure 3-3. Packed bullion stitches (see Figure 6-6).

Figure 3-4. Many hours of patient effort resulted in this unique necklace. The American Indian basket technique was used to form the circles, which were sewn together and inset with shisha mirrors. Designed by Carol Martin.

The beautiful coiled necklace shown in Figure 3-4 took hours and hours to make, but was well worth the effort. The designer began by sketching her design in order to achieve the correct balance of large and small circles. Using very fine jute as the core, she wrapped the jute with cotton, silk, and wool in shades of mauve. A tiny bit of silver metallic thread was used in the wrapping to repeat the silver of the mirrors. She used the Figure-8 coiling method (see *Techniques of Basketry*, by Virginia Harvey, Van Nostrand Reinhold,© 1974). Only natural fibers were used, since man-made fibers (acrylic, nylon, etc.) tend to stretch in the wrapping process. Make the neckband first, remembering to leave a loop for a button closure at the back of the neck. After forming each circle separately, add mirrors in the centers of an occasional circle. Slip-stitch the circles together and attach them to the choker. You can keep adding circles as your time and patience permit.

Footgear

Believe it or not, mirror embroidery can be used to spruce up your feet. A variety of embroidery stitches was used to encircle the mirrors on a pair of zany, mirrored socks (see Figure 3-5). (On any item with as much "give" as socks, the framework mesh over the mirrors must be done snugly, but the surrounding embroidery is done with a looser tension.) And, while red espadrilles are pretty spiffy all alone, one designer made them dazzling with her own version of embroidery and mirrors (see Figure 3-6). With one skein each of D.M.C. six-strand embroidery floss in turquoise, hot pink, orange, and yellow, the mirrors were attached with the cretan stitch method (see Figure 1-2). Lazy daisies, buttonholes, and French knots surround the mirrors. Canvas shoes can be tricky to work on (especially near the toes), but pliers and a curved carpet needle can make the embroidery process easier.

Floral-Motif Purse (see Figure 3-9)

Materials:

½ yard of white linen fabric for front and back of bag

½ yard of lining fabric

Sewing thread

Seven shisha mirrors

One skein each of D.M.C. pearl cotton, size #3, in chartreuse, dark orange, and light orange

One skein of D.M.C. pearl cotton, size #5, in medium orange

One skein each of Glosilla® by Bucilla in goldenrod and magenta

Two wood handles with long slits

Directions:

1.   From purse fabric, cut one piece, 12 by 28 inches for the front and back, and two pieces, each 7¼ inches long by 4¼ inches wide at the bottom end and 3 inches wide at the top. Cut the same size pieces from the lining fabric. From purse fabric cut two 3- by 28-inch pieces for straps.

2.   On the wrong side of the main purse piece draw a chalk line across the center from one long edge to the other. Also, on the wrong side mark the center of the bottom edge of each gusset. On the right side of the lining main piece draw a line parallel to and 6 inches from the short edge.

3.   Using the pattern in Figure 3-10, transfer the design onto the right side of your main purse piece, using either dressmaker's carbon or a hectograph pencil.

4.   Embroider the design, placing mirrors in the circled areas and attaching them with one row of buttonhole stitching. Fill in the rest of the design with satin stitches in D.M.C. pearl cotton, Glosilla® by Bucilla, and six-strand embroidery floss. See Figure 3-11 for a detail of the textures made by the various stitches.

5.   With right sides together and raw edges even, pin the bottom edge of one gusset to a side edge of the bag main piece, matching the center mark and chalk line. Stitch across the gusset, starting and stopping ½ inch from the sides; knot thread ends. Clip bag seam allowance opposite the knots. Swivel the bag fabric at the clips and pin together at the side edges of the bag and gusset. Stitch up the sides. Repeat for the other gusset and then repeat for the lining.

Figure 3-11. Detail of satin stitching done on the Floral-Motif Purse shown in Figure 3-9. Various textures were achieved by using a variety of embroidery threads.

Figure 3-12. Persian purses were made from scraps of richly hued velvet, metallic threads, and tassels. The timy mirrors add an exotic touch. Designed by Maureen Flores.

Fancier Bags

For fancier bags, the Persian purses (see Figure 3-12) make perfect accessories for evening wear. They are just large enough for a lipstick, keys, and a small comb. The designer used two pieces of old-gold color velvet, approximately 5 by 7 inches each. She also used two pieces of silk, in the same color and size, for the lining. Using D.M.C. pearl cotton, size #5, in a combination of red, pink, orange, purple, and magenta, she made cretans, open chains and chain stitches around the mirrors. Gold metallic thread was used for more interest. Tiny little "dancing bells" dot the corners. The cord handle was made by braiding D.M.C. pearl cotton, size #3, and attaching to the purse with whipstitches. See page 71 for instructions on how to make the eye-catching tassels.

Apron and Belt

If your husband calls at the last minute to tell you that he's bringing his boss home for dinner, tie on a sparkling apron (see Color Plate 29) and, if you're lucky, no one will notice that they're eating last night's leftovers with a can of mushroom soup poured over the top! The belt shown in Figure 3-13 is an ideal choice to be worn with the apron.

Hostess Apron (see Figure 3-13)
Materials:

1¼ yards of heavy, bright pink cotton fabric (45 inches wide)

Small amounts of lightweight cotton fabric in gold (color A), green (B), purple (C), orange (D), blue (E), dark red (F), and light red (G)

Eleven skeins of six-strand embroidery floss in the following colors and quantities: three skeins red (H), three skeins purple (C), two skeins yellow (I), two skeins orange (D), one skein blue (E)

90 yards Persian-type needlepoint or crewel yarn in the following colors and quantities: 60 yards dark turquoise (J), 30 yards light green (K)

Thirty-two shisha mirrors

Size:
About 39 inches long

Figure 3-13. Detail of the Hostess Belt and Apron.

Directions:

1. From pink cotton cut 30- by 40-inch rectangle for apron, a 5- by 24-inch strip for waistband, and two 5- by 36-inch strips for ties. Enlarge the diagram in Figure 3-14 and transfer to the appropriate color fabric. Cut each appliqué piece as indicated on patterns, adding ½-inch seam allowance to all edges. Cut full shapes where they overlap and cut only one pattern for similar shapes, such as hearts and circles of the same size and petals. Do not cut S or M circles; S circles will be embroidered in satin stitches later and M circles are for the mirrors. Turn under and press seams on appliqué pieces, clipping curved edges.

2. Attach a mirror to the center of each M circle on appliqué pieces along the center fold of apron, following Figure 3-14 for floss indicated on the circle. For M–H and M–I circles work ⅜-inch-long blanket stitches over framework. Then around the M–H circles work another round of blanket stitches in color H. For M–D and M–C circles work ⅜-inch long-legged cretan stitch over framework. Then around the M–C circles work a round of blanket stitches in color E.

3. Starting 4 inches from waist edge, assemble and appliqué pieces along the center fold of apron, following Figure 3-13 for placement. Mark and embroider S circles in satin stitch with color I floss. With color J wool embroider a French knot on each dot on the large circles. Attach M–J mirrors and work ⅜-inch-long blanket stitches with color J wool around them.

4. Make ½-inch finished hems along sides of apron and make a 2-inch hem at the lower edge. Gather waist edge of apron to measure 18 inches, leaving the center 9 inches flat. With right sides facing and raw edges matching, center one long edge of waistband across top edge of apron; stitch. Fold band in half to wrong side, turn under seam on other long edge, and blindstitch. Turn in raw ends of bands. Fold a tie in half lengthwise, wrong side out. Cut one end at angle. Seam angled end and long edge. Turn, insert raw end in the end of waistband; topstitch. Seam and attach other tie in the same manner.

Figure 3-14. Pattern for the Hostess Apron shown in Color Plate 29. Designed by Marilyn Wein. Reprinted by permission of *Woman's Day* magazine © 1974 by Fawcett Publications, Inc.

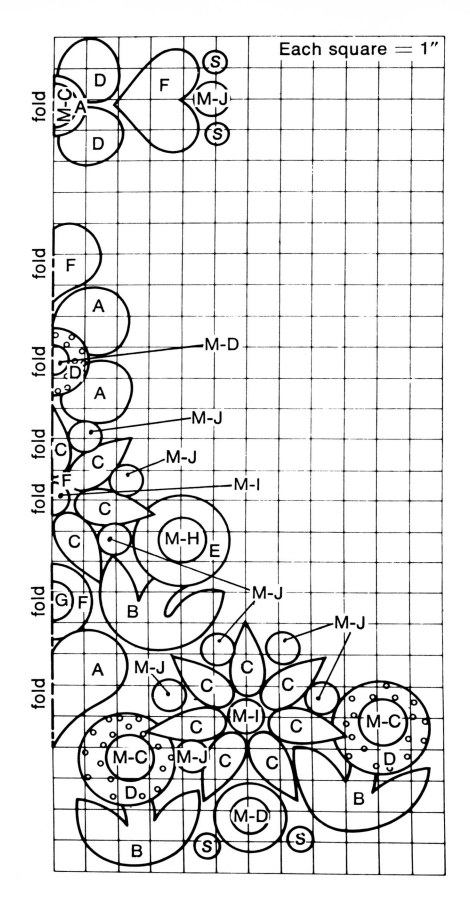

Each square = 1"

A = gold cotton

B = green cotton

C = purple cotton

D = orange cotton

E = blue cotton

F = dark red cotton

G = red cotton

H = red floss

C = purple floss

I = yellow floss

O = orange floss

E = blue floss

J = turquoise crewel yarn

K = light green crewel yarn

M = mirror

S = satin stitch

Hostess Belt (see Figure 3-13)
Materials:
⅛ yard of bright yellow felt
¼ yard of bright orange felt
60 yards each of Persian-type needlepoint yarn in bright pink,
 orange, light green, and turquoise
One ball of pearl cotton, size #5, in orange
Small strips of Velcro® for closing
Two hooks and eyes
Ten shisha mirrors
Jingle jangles
Three wool pom-poms

Size:
3¼ feet wide

Directions:
1.   Enlarge Figure 3-15, extending scalloped edges to measure 31 inches (see Sketch 1). Take your waist measurement. If necessary, adjust pattern length to desired size (end X overlaps end Y by 1 inch), as follows: Trace your drawing, adding a little space between mirrors for a longer belt or taking out a little space for a shorter one; make sure spaces between mirrors are the same (for 3-inch shorter belt, omit one mirror and embroider a scallop at end X). This is your adjusted pattern.
2.   Cut orange felt for backing from pattern, adding 1-inch tab at end Y. Cut yellow felt for belt front, adding ½-inch seams all around.

3.   Lightly mark outlines of mirrors along yellow felt. For embroidery use two strands of wool throughout. In the first circle to be embroidered, work satin stitch in areas A in pink and then satin stitch in green in circle B. Work green satin stitch in circle B, turquoise French knots in areas C and turquoise French knots in areas D. In the next circle to be embroidered, work turquoise satin stitch in circle B, turquoise French knots in areas C, and green French knots in areas D. Alternate colors in this manner across the belt.
4.   Turn under seams on yellow felt; blindstitch to orange backing. Sew strips of Velcro® at ends. Glue mirrors in place.
5.   Arrange pom-poms and jingle jangles as shown in Sketch 2 (Figure 3-15), with ends overlapping. For ease in handling, glue together just enough to hold them in one piece. Wrap together just very tightly with orange pearl cotton. Thread end in needle and run through wrappings to hold. Sew eye to each end. Sew hooks to correspond on wrong side of belt front.

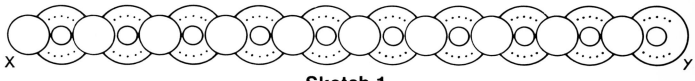

X   Y

Sketch 1

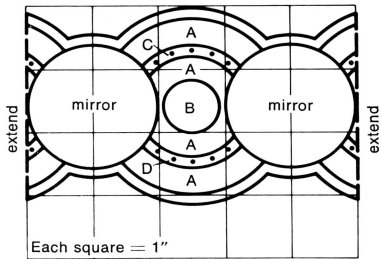

extend   mirror   A C   A   B   A   D   A   mirror   extend

Each square = 1"

Pattern for Belt

Figure 3-15. Pattern for the Hostess Belt shown in Figure *3-13.*

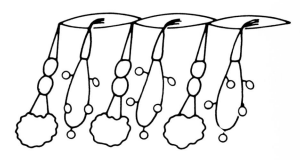

Sketch 2

Tassels

Tassels are the exclamation points on handmade treasures. Think beyond the corners of pillows and try tassels on a sleeve, as a necklace, as a zipper pull, as drapery swags, as the pull chains in posh powder rooms, or in giant clusters on luggage handles. (This would certainly make your plain blue Samsonite stand out in the sea of suitcases at the airport.)

Tassels range from the simple, which only take a few minutes to make, to the elaborately elegant, which can take hours, days, or weeks, depending upon how fanciful you feel. You can bead and bejewel them, you can wrap and braid them, you can comb and trim them and, of course, most of mine are mirrored. For centuries tassels have been used in a myriad of ways—on tapestries in the Middle East, on camels in Egypt, on bellpulls in England, and on cardinals in Rome.

Basic Tassels

Tassels can be made from embroidery floss, rayon chainette, rug yarn, or twisted wool yarns. The amount needed depends on the size of your tassel. You'll also need a piece of sturdy cardboard, scissors, and a needle.

In Figure 3-16 the various steps of making a tassel are illustrated. Cut a piece of cardboard the same length as you want your finished tassel to be. Wrap yarn neatly around the cardboard (Step 1). If you want a plump tassel, wrap many times. Cut a piece of yarn about 36 inches long. Tie the cut ends together with a small knot. Placing either an index finger or a pencil in each end of the loop (the knot should be in between the loops in the center), twist one end away from you and one end toward you, until it begins to kink and twist together in the center (Step 2). Grasp both ends in one hand and drop the other end. The cord will twist itself together. With the index finger of your free hand, adjust the rope by sliding your index finger between the two cords, evening the twist (Step 3). Slip the twisted cord under the wrapped yarn, slide it to the top, and tie a secure knot (Step 4). Using a sharp pair of scissors, cut along the bottom of the cardboard and remove the tassel from the cardboard (Step 5). Turn the knotted cord down to the underside of the tassel (Step 6). Taking another piece of yarn, wrap securely around the tassel (Step 7). Finish wrapping by using a needle, as shown (Step 8). Tie a knot (Step 9). You now have a basic tassel which can be left as is or embellished.

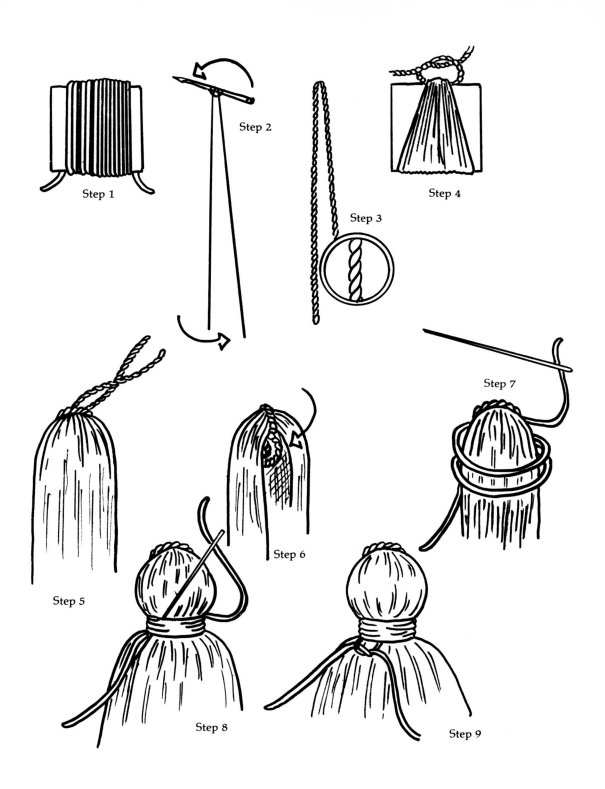

Step 1

Step 2

Step 3

Step 4

Step 5

Step 6

Step 7

Step 8

Step 9

Figure 3-16. The basic tassel.

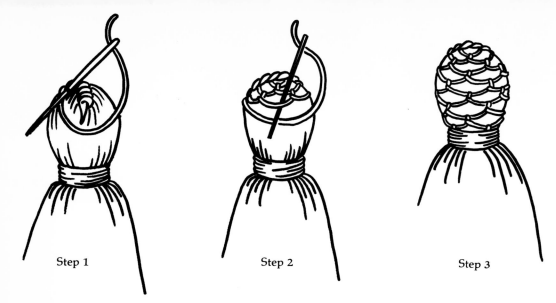

Step 1   Step 2   Step 3

Loop Method

Figure 3-17-A and -B. Ruth Colt uses the loop method and the intersection method to make her tassels.

Embellished Tassels

One way to embellish a tassel is to do the buttonhole stitch around the head of the tassel (see Figure 3-17-A). For the "loop" method thread a long piece of yarn (either the same yarn or a contrasting color) onto a needle and hide the knot by coming up from the underside of the tassel, and then up and out through the top of the tassel head. Do one row of buttonhole stitching, with stitches very close together, around the top of the tassel (Step 1). Continue around the tassel (Step 2), going into each loop. Your needle should not hook into the yarn on the head of the tassel. The detached buttonhole stitches are a netting, so to speak, and are only attached top and bottom. (Step 3 shows the results of inserting the needle into every loop.)

Another way to embellish the basic tassel is shown in Figure 3-17-B. Hide the knot by coming up and out of the top of the tassel and make a row of detached buttonhole stitches with stitches worked very close together around the top (Step 1). In the second and remaining rows insert the needle at the intersection. This produces a different effect (Step 3).

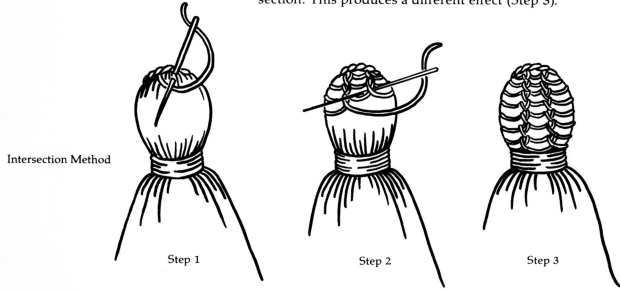

Intersection Method

Step 1   Step 2   Step 3

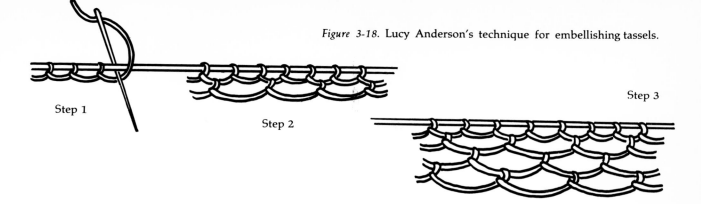

Figure 3-18. Lucy Anderson's technique for embellishing tassels.

Step 1

Step 2

Step 3

Step 4

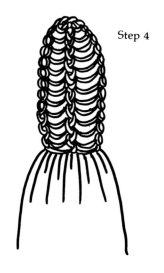

Still another way of embellishing tassels is shown in Figure 3-18. Do a single row of buttonhole stitches, worked very close together, around the top of the tassel (Step 1). On the second row only skip every other loop (Step 2). Be careful not to let your needle hook into the yarn on the head of the tassel. For the third and remaining rows insert your needle into every loop (Step 3). (The completed tassel is shown in Step 4.) Notice how the ridges predominate the embellished head of the tassel (see Figure 3-19). The tassels in Figure 3-20 were made using various tensions to pull the buttonhole stitching, and still another idea is the tassel in Figure 3-21, which is made of embroidery floss and tiny "shinies." The twisted cord was left to show instead of being turned to the inside of the tassel.

Figure 3-21. Gwenn Stutzman used embroidery floss and small "shinies" for her tiny tassel.

Figure 3-19. Lucy Anderson made this necklace from a tiny tassel. The yarn tassel complements the heavier-weight imported wool top on which she has stitched mirrors.

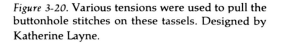

Figure 3-20. Various tensions were used to pull the buttonhole stitches on these tassels. Designed by Katherine Layne.

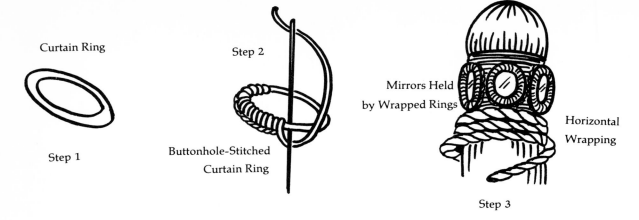

Curtain Ring

Step 1

Step 2

Buttonhole-Stitched
Curtain Ring

Mirrors Held
by Wrapped Rings

Horizontal
Wrapping

Step 3

Figure 3-22. Ruth Colt's method of embellishing tassels with wrapped rings and horizontal wraps covered with vertical wraps.

Wrapped Tassels

An interesting approach to decorating tassels is shown in Figure 3-22. Take a tiny plastic curtain ring, slightly smaller in size than the shisha mirror (Step 1) and do the buttonhole stitch all around it (Step 2). Hold a shisha mirror onto the head of the tassel and place the wrapped ring on top of the shisha mirror, thus holding the shisha mirror in place. Using a needle and thread, make small whipstitches here and there, until the wrapped ring (and the mirror beneath it) is securely tacked to the head of the tassel. Use several rings to hold on several mirrors (Step 3). Then wrap around the tassel several times, horizontally, using thick yarn, thus forming a bulge. Wrap still another thread, vertically, until all of the thick yarn underneath is covered (Step 4). Always be sure to work from the top of the tassel down.

The elaborately wrapped tassel in Figure 3-23 is made with a combination of wool, metallic, and glossy threads. Note that various shapes have been achieved by doing horizontal wraps and then covering them over with vertical wrappings. Area A was made by dividing the yarn into vertical strands and wrapping each bunch separately. Chain and cretan stitches were added for further embellishment. Another ingenious tassel is shown in Figure 3-24. It was made from wool rug yarn. The head of the tassel was covered with detached buttonhole stitches, and horizontal wraps and then vertical wraps were used to embellish the tassel. Tiny coins provide the finishing touches.

Vertical
Wrapping

Step 4

Result

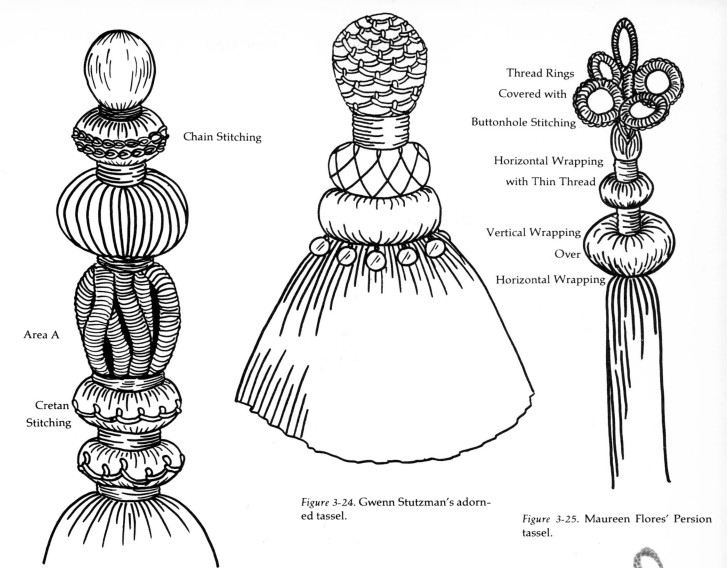

Chain Stitching

Area A

Cretan
Stitching

Figure 3-23. Maureen Flores' wrapped
tassel.

Thread Rings
Covered with

Buttonhole Stitching

Horizontal Wrapping
with Thin Thread

Vertical Wrapping
Over

Horizontal Wrapping

Figure 3-24. Gwenn Stutzman's adorned tassel.

Figure 3-25. Maureen Flores' Persion
tassel.

Figure 3-26. This "pyramid tassel" was
made by attaching three tin-framed
mirrors to the head of a basic tassel.
Designed by Lucy Anderson.

Persian Tassels

Tiny Persian tassels like the one shown in Figure 3-25 were
made to enhance the Persian purses shown in Figure 3-12.
Make the individual top circles, or rings, by wrapping thread
around your finger several times, and, while the thread is still
on your finger, do the buttonhole stitch over the thread. Be
careful not to poke your finger with the needle! After you have
done the buttonhole stitch all the way around the thread ring,
snip the thread. Attach several thread rings together and attach them to the top of the tassel. Continue embellishing the
tassel, being sure to work from the top down. Use a combination of shiny, metallic and matte-finish threads.

Assorted Tassels

Holes were poked in the edges of three tin-frame mirrors.
They were then sewn together and attached to the top of the
tassel head (see Figure 3-26). A great variety of tassels were
used on the bottom of the sun banner shown in Figure 4-8.
These tassels were made using a variety of techniques (see

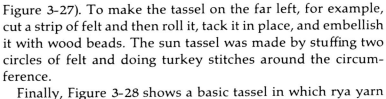

Figure 3-27. Detail of the tassels shown on the sun banner in Figure 4-8. A variety of techniques were used to make the tassels. Designed by Phyllis Hall.

Figure 3-27). To make the tassel on the far left, for example, cut a strip of felt and then roll it, tack it in place, and embellish it with wood beads. The sun tassel was made by stuffing two circles of felt and doing turkey stitches around the circumference.

Finally, Figure 3-28 shows a basic tassel in which rya yarn was used. The detached buttonhole was done around the head of the tassel, and then pom-poms and tiny metal beads were added.

Figure 3-28. This basic tassel was made with rya rug yarn and then adorned with pom-poms, tiny metal beads, and bells. Designed by Jeannie Anderson.

Figure 4-1. This white linen pillow was embellished with amber mirrors and entitled "Reflections." Designed by the author as a kit for Bucilla.

4

Interior Reflections

We often hear "Your home is your castle." If *your* castle is looking more like a dreary dungeon, don't despair! With a pillow here, a banner there, a quilt to catch your eye, you can give personality to your same old palace. Whether we live in an efficiency apartment or a gated mansion, our homes, like the clothes we wear, tell a lot about us. Most importantly, we must be comfortable with, and in, our surroundings. Even in this age of mass-produced furnishings, we can make our homes unique and let our personalities shine through with the little delights we add.

Pillows

Pillows aren't just for sleeping upon! Small ones can be placed on couches or large ones tossed on the floor. They can completely change the mood of your room. The white linen pillow shown in Figure 4-1 is a case in point. The pillow simply consists of amber mirrors surrounded by satin-stitched flowers (see Figure 4-2), but its impact is strong. Two pieces of white linen, approximately 16 inches square, are used for the front and back. Four skeins each of mustard, old gold, orange, and moss green Glosilla® by Bucilla were used to complete the design. The mirrors were attached using the cretan stitch method (see Figure 1-2). Densely spaced satin stitches encompass the mirror, forming the flower petal shapes, while the leaves were done in the fishbone stitch.

Figure 4-2. Detail of the embroidered flower on the pillow shown in Figure 4-1. Satin and fishbone stitches were used to encompass the mirror.

Figure 4-3. Hexagon shapes were cut from a variety of fabrics, stitched together, and then spaced satin stitches, mirrors, and bells were added to create these unusual pillows. Designed by Lucy Anderson.

Figure 4-4. Mirrors are the stars in the sky on this "Man In The Moon" pillow by Mary Hardy. Three shades of blue felt, pearl cotton, mirrors, and lots of imagination are the ingredients.

A patchwork technique was used to make the pillow shown in Figure 4-3. Any patchwork technique can be used, but here the designer used hexagons. The pillow is approximately 17 by 17 inches and was made from plain and printed cotton fabrics in shades of mauve and purple. The straight stitches and mirror attachments were done in six-strand embroidery floss. Approximately two skeins each of cranberry, wine, purple, mauve, cinnamon, and plum were needed. Little "dancing bells" dot the outside angles of the pillow. The nice thing about this type of pillow is that you don't have to be quite so careful sewing your patches together when you know there will be embroidery over the seams!

A completely different effect was achieved with appliquéd felt (see Figure 4-4). "Man in the Moon" was made from three shades of blue felt, and shisha mirrors were used for the stars in the sky. The designer constructed this pillow by first cutting out two circles of dark blue felt, 18 inches in diameter. She then cut two half-moons—one in medium blue and one in sky blue. The face detail was embroidered onto the sky blue half-moon, and it was placed on the medium blue half-moon so that ½ to ¾ inches of the medium blue border showed. The designer then attached both half-moons to the dark blue circle with a running stitch. Shisha mirrors were randomly stitched on for the stars using a variety of stitches. French knots were added around the mirrors in the same color as the mirror stitching. The right sides were then put together, stitched, turned, and stuffed. Scenes such as this one make attractive wall hangings and banners, as well. One skein each of D.M.C. pearl cotton, size #5, in navy, royal, and medium and light blue was used for the embroidery and mirror attachment.

Chairs

Shisha mirrors provide a grand solution to an old problem. Cigarette holes left by careless smokers in dining room chairs can be beautifully and creatively concealed by shisha mirror embroidery. Here's another solution to another old problem—sore backs from ladder-back dining room chairs. One designer remedied this with trapuntoed, embroidered, and mirrored chair-back pads (see Figure 4-5). Now she and her family dine in beauty and comfort. The heavy cotton rose-colored fabric was stuffed with polyester batting and the whole pad is machine washable. The embroidery stitches used include van dykes, chains, buttonholes, spiderwebs, French knots, long-legged French knots, straight stitches, and detached chains. One skein each of the following colors of six-strand embroidery floss was used: medium green, black, coral, red, medium gold, and bright blue.

Quilts

Revive old quilts and coverlets with shisha mirror embroidery. The mirrors can be incorporated into just about any print design—florals, geometrics, stripes—or can be attractively arranged on solids.

The quilt shown in Figure 4-6 and Color Plate 21 was made with bright Marimekko cotton fabric that I spotted while shopping and couldn't resist. I decided to make a quilt out of the fabric—I had purchased 1 yard each of seven pieces—and, as is so often the case, shisha mirrors provided just the right decorator touch. To make the quilt, I first carefully cut 7-inch squares from the yards of fabric. (I used 336 squares for a twin-sized spread.) Sitting on the floor (the only place large enough), I arranged the squares in a pleasing pattern. I was then ready to sew the squares together. I picked up the squares, one horizontal row at a time, stitched and pressed open the ¼-inch seams. Next, all of the rows were stitched together. Between the backing (a complementary colored Marimekko sheet) and the patchwork top I placed four layers of batting. Each corner of each square was tied with D.M.C. pearl cotton, size #3, to give a quilted effect. The tin-frame mirrors were then added with the bits of Velcro® so that they could be easily removed for cleaning.

Figure 4-5. Alexis Wright combined trapunto and mirror embroidery to form padded cushions for the backs of her dining room chairs.

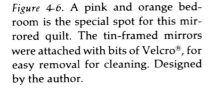

Figure 4-6. A pink and orange bedroom is the special spot for this mirrored quilt. The tin-framed mirrors were attached with bits of Velcro®, for easy removal for cleaning. Designed by the author.

Figure 4-8. Shisha mirrors accent the rays of sun on this striking felt banner. Detail of the imaginative tassels are shown in Figure 3-27. Designed by Phyllis Hall.

Figure 4-7. Four-inch squares of fabric were individually batiked in circular designs. They were then sewn together, and a mirror accents the center of each square to make this spectacular banner. Designed by Carol Martin. Ruth Colt made the tassel that hangs from the upper lefthand corner.

Banners

There are countless numbers of ways to use banners. They can be hung outside to greet party guests, they can signify a special event, or they can be hung inside or outside simply for fun. They're a kind of celebration unto themselves!

For the banner shown in Figure 4-7, individual squares of cotton muslin fabric were batiked in a wheel design and were dyed in tones of magenta and orange. The squares were then stitched together and a mirror was sewn in the center of each. One skein each of D.M.C. pearl cotton, size #5, and size #8, in red, orange, magenta, hot pink, purple, and mauve were used to stitch on the mirrors using the cretan stitch method (see Figure 1-2) and the buttonhole method (see Figure 1-3). French knots were added for textural interest and a special tassel was made to hang in the upper left-hand corner. Tassels are perfect too for the sun banner shown in Figure 4-8. Shisha mirrors were effectively used as the rays of the sun. The sun was made from pieces of yellow and orange felt, which were padded and machine-stitched onto the black felt background. Black D.M.C. pearl cotton, size #5, was used for the outline stitch that forms the face detail. Between the felt sun rays are outline stitches done in D.M.C. pearl cotton, size #5, in yellow and orange shades. The mirrors were attached using the buttonhole stitch and cretan stitch method (see Figures 1-2 and 1-3), again with D.M.C. pearl cotton, size #5. An assortment of decorative tassels was added to the bottom of the banner. See Figure 3-27 for a detailed view of these tassels.

Shisha mirrors add striking accents to banners with religious themes. Felt, ribbons, a tiny butterfly mola, and shisha mirrors were used to create the banner shown in Figure 4-9. It is entitled "Tonight is Born the Children's King." The colors used in the banner are purple, red, orange, and hot pink. It was made predominantly from felt, and the mirrors were attached using D.M.C. pearl cotton, size #5, in the cretan stitch method (see Figure 1-2). The butterfly was used to symbolize fertility and life, and the multicolored satin ribbon streamers add just the right festive touch.

Accessories

Boxes are perfect hiding places for jewelry, trinkets, or other good things, and make fine decorative accessories for your tables or chests, as well. Once again, shisha mirrors add magic and charm.

Figure 4-9. A contemporary religious banner was designed by Jorjanna Lundgren. Ribbon streamers were hung from the felt to signify celebration, and the words "Tonight is Born The Children's King" were appliquèd in felt.

Figure 4-10. Debbie Keith created this imaginative soft sculpture box decorated with her adaptation of a verse by Goethe. Her box reads, "To know someone here or there with whom you can feel there is understanding, in spite of distance or thoughts unexpressed, that can make of this earth a garden."

The beautiful soft sculpture fabric box (see Figure 4-10) was inspired by Goethe's verse "To know someone whom we accord with, who is living on with us, even in silence—this makes our earthly ball a peopled garden." (*Apprenticeship Wilhelm Meister's Lehrjahre*, Book VII, chapter 5, 1786–1830.) The designer has freely adapted the verse to read "To know someone here or there, with whom you can feel there is understanding, in spite of distances or thoughts unexpressed, can make of this earth a garden." The entire 5½-inch box was hand-stitched. The letters on the box were cut out of fabrics and stitched on using tiny whipstitches. Even the interior of the box (see Figure 4-11) has been beautifully decorated with intricately stitched mirrors. The bottom of the box (see Figure 4-12) features a mirror surrounded by a raised and padded circle. Details of the lettering around the box are shown in

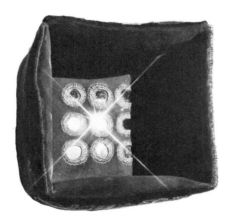

Figure 4-11. Detail of the interior of the fabric box shown in Figure 4-10. Notice the intricate stitching of the shisha mirrors.

Figure 4-12. Detail of the bottom side of the box shown in Figure 4-10. A mirror is surrounded by a velvet padded mound.

Figure 4-13. The "To know someone" side of the box.

Figure 4-14. "Understanding" is shown on this side of the box.

Figures 4-13 through 4-16. The colors are American beauty red, rust, orange, magenta, purple, black, and light rose pink. D.M.C. pearl cotton, sizes #5, and #8, were used for the stitching.

Though it might seem unlikely at first, shisha mirror embroidery is a perfect way to decorate baskets. Since most baskets are obviously difficult to sew through, a good technique to use is to first sew mirrors onto a piece or strip of fabric and then baste or glue the fabric onto the basket. Actually, there's no end to the possibilities in this area. On the Persian basket shown in Figure 4-17, gold metallic threads and high luster threads in shades of magenta, red, orange, and purple were wrapped over jute in the American Indian basket technique. (See *Techniques of Basketry,* by Virginia Harvey, Van Nostrand Reinhold, © 1974.) Small shisha mirrors and bugle beads (rectangular, glass beads) were sewn onto fabric using D.M.C. pearl cotton, size #5, in matching colors. The fabric piece was then basted onto the top of the basket, and upholstery fringe was added around the lid for a finishing touch.

Fancy book bindings can dress up a nightstand, and shisha mirrors can dress up the bindings. Felt, lace, and mirrors were used to bind the book shown in Figure 4-18. The monogram adds a personal touch. Bindings should be removable, so that you can change the book inside and keep the same beautiful cover.

Figure 4-15. The "distance or thoughts" side of the box.

Figure 4-16. "Garden" with a sparkling shisha mirror is shown on one side of the box.

Figure 4-17. Maureen Flores made a tiny Persion basket by wrapping high luster yarns and gold thread over jute. The basket can be a hiding place for tiny treasures

Figure 4-18. Felt, bits of lace, and shisha mirrors were used to decorate and monogram a book binding. Designed by Mary Hardy.

Holiday Decorations

When it's time to deck the halls and your traditional tinsel is tarnished, add some new sparkle! From the tiniest ornament to the most elaborate wreath, the whole family can participate in making your holiday mantel magnificent. Shisha mirrors help the festivities get underway.

An easy ornament to construct is the stocking shown in Figure 4-19. The jingle jangles and pom-poms hanging from the top left are optional, but they do add a festive touch to the stocking. The jingle jangles are simply metal discs attached to silk loops. They make a divine tinkling sound and, combined with pom-poms from India, they are a handsome addition to the stocking.

Christmas Stocking (see Figure 4–19)
Materials:
One 12- by 16-inch piece of orange felt for front or back stocking piece
One 12- by 16-inch piece of magenta felt for front or back stocking piece
One 12- by 12-inch piece of magenta felt for the three flowers, top piece, and toe piece
One skein each of D.M.C. pearl cotton, size #5, in orange and hot pink
Six tin-frame mirrors
Wood beads in a variety of shapes
Optional: pom-poms and jingle jangles for tassel
½ foot of ¾-inch wide grosgrain ribbon in magenta for the hanger

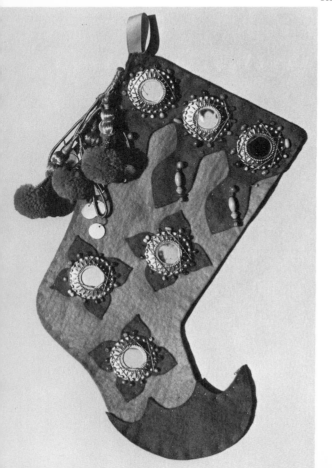

Figure 4-19. The festive Christmas Stocking was made from two shades of felt, tin-framed mirrors, pearl cotton, and wood beads. Designed by Judy Stoup.

Directions:

1. Enlarge the stocking pattern shown in Figure 4-20. Using the pattern, cut a front stocking piece from one color of felt, a back stocking piece from another color of felt, and the top, toe, and flower shapes from the 12-inch magenta piece of felt.
2. Using D.M.C. pearl cotton, size #5, and a small running stitch, hand-stitch the top scalloped piece, the flowers, and the toe piece to the front piece only of the stocking. Using a dab of white glue, attach the tin-frame mirrors to the center of each flower shape. Using D.M.C. pearl cotton, size #5, make a network of straight stitches to secure the tin-frame mirrors (see Figure 4-19).
3. Using D.M.C. pearl cotton, size #5, attach beads (see page 33).
4. Hand-stitch front and back stocking pieces together.
5. Wrap the jingle jangles and pom-poms together as shown in Figure 3-15.
6. Tack on the loop of grosgrain ribbon and hang in a special spot.

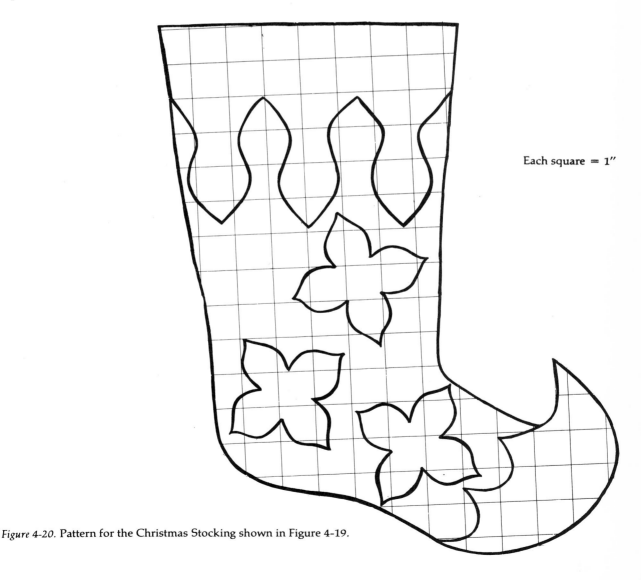

Each square = 1″

Figure 4-20. Pattern for the Christmas Stocking shown in Figure 4-19.

Figure 4-21. Hundreds of stuffed fabric balls form the gay Christmas Wreath. Shisha mirrors dot some of the tufts. Ribbons can be hung like streamers from the wreath, if you wish. Designed by the author.

Christmas Wreath (*see Figure 4–21*)
Materials:
3 yards each of cotton fabric in magenta, orange, and red
600 to 900 cotton balls (or save lint from your dryer), depending upon how puffy you want the fabric balls to be
Rubber bands
Florist's picks or large toothpicks
Hay or Styrofoam wreath
Fifty shisha mirrors or as many as you wish
One skein each of D.M.C. pearl cotton, size #5, in red and orange

Directions:
1.   Use a plate with a 5-inch diameter to trace the circles. Place the plate on the fabric and trace around the circumference with a pencil. Continue tracing circles, making them as close together as possible , and then cut them out.
2.   In Figure 4-22 the following steps are illustrated: Using pearl cotton, stitch a mirror in the center of as many circles as you desire (Step 1). Place a large tuft of cotton in the center of a circle of fabric (Step 2). Then scrunch it up and tightly wrap with a rubber band. Either wire it onto a florist's pick or place it on a large toothpick (Step 3). Place all of the balls into the hay wreath, putting them as close together as possible (Step 4). The completed wreath is shown in Step 5.

Step 1

Step 2

Step 3

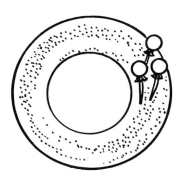

Step 4

Result

Figure 4-22. Making the Christmas Wreath.

More Ornaments

The clever ornament shown in Figure 4-23 was made by taking a semicircle of #12 mono needlepoint canvas, working it in various stitches, shaping it into a cone, and then tacking to secure it in the shape. Persian yarn in shades of scarlet, rust, orange, brick red, magenta, royal blue, turquoise, burnt sienna, and flesh color were used for the ornament. A row of blue shisha mirrors was added around the lower edge, using the cretan stitch method (see Figure 1-2). After, the beard was stitched on with orange yarn in the turkey work stitch. A tiny music box was placed inside (see Supplier's list at the back of the book).

Another creative use of odds and ends is seen in figure 4-24. To make this circle tree ornament, you'll need a lid from a tin can for the core of the ornament, a circle of felt or leather for the backing, a circle of #10 mono needlepoint canvas, metallic threads in a variety of colors — blue, red, copper, silver, green (see Supplier's list at the back of the book) — shisha mirrors, and tiny bells. The designer randomly painted on the needlepoint canvas with red and blue acrylic paints. She then wove metallic threads over and under the canvas threads. She also did some diagonal tents for concentrated stitching. The mirrors were attached using straight spoke stitches, and some mirrors were further embellished with areas of over-and-under weaving. Bells were tacked on last. Let your imagination go wild on this project and stitch to your hearts content!

Figure 4-23. A music box was tucked inside this sparkling Santa Claus, and blue mirrors accent the lower edge of Santa. The beard is a turkey loop stitching in yarn. Designed by Kay Whitcombe.

Figure 4-24. A tin can lid was transformed into a unique Christmas tree ornament by Ruth Colt. Metallic threads cover the needlepoint canvas, and the ornament was backed with felt.

Figure 5-1. Alexis Wright created this design to be used as the bodice for her Afghani Nomad dress. (See Color Plate 15.)

5

Symmetrical Designs

The way shape, color, or texture is used determines whether or not the design is balanced. In embroidery, as in other media, it is important to achieve the proper juxtaposition of these elements of design (shape, color, texture, etc.) so that the result is pleasing to the eye. For the novice properly balancing a design can be difficult. Using a symmetrical design that is already balanced can be a safe and esthetically pleasing solution. The greatest advantage to using a symmetrical design is that you can concentrate on your stitches and colors, rather than on the creation of the design itself. In using the symmetrical design outlines that follow you can make them as simple or as elaborate as you wish by varying the amount of stitchery you use as filler. Perhaps after you've had some experience with symmetrical designs you'll feel inspired to create your own. In either case, the following techniques of enlarging and transferring apply.

Enlarging

The designs in this chapter can be used as is or can be enlarged or reduced as your need demands. For a nominal fee the local blueprinter can reduce or enlarge the design with equipment while you wait. If you wish, however, enlarge the designs yourself by transferring them onto a 1-inch grid paper or paper that you have drawn a 1-inch grid upon. Then copy the design onto the grid square by square.

Figure 5-2. Pattern for the design shown in Figure 5-1.

Figure 5-3. The Afghani Nomad dress. Folkwear Pattern #107 gives instructions for embroidery, stitching on mirrors, and making the dress.

Tracing

Using a hectograph pencil (see Supplier's list at the back of the book) is an other excellent way to transfer a design. With pen or pencil trace the pattern on paper of good quality. Then trace over the design with the hectograph pencil. Put the side of the paper that you've marked *face down* onto the fabric and, with a hot iron, press the design. Hectograph pencils are made in both purple and yellow, but the purple one seems to work better.

Designs

The design in Figure 5-1 and Color Plate 15 was created for the bodice of an Afghani Nomad dress. These dresses are the traditional dress of tribal women of Afghanistan. They are full skirted, ankle length, and have tight fitting bodices open at the back of the neck. The sleeves usually have three sections, each section in a different fabric.

The symmetrical design is shown in Figure 5-2, and the Afghani Nomad dress is shown in Figure 5-3. After making the basic dress in shades of purple and mauve cotton from a Folkwear Pattern (see Supplier's list in the back of the book), the designer transferred her original design onto the bodice. Using two skeins each of D. M. C. embroidery floss in crimson, old gold, plum, green, purple, and aqua, she then did the satin, chain, spiderweb, outline, lazy daisy, buttonhole, Pekinese, laced cretan, couching, and herringbone stitches to fill in the design. Mirrors surrounded by stitching (see Alexis Wright's method, Figure 1-7), were placed on the sleeves (see Figure 5-4).

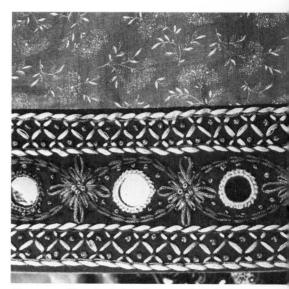

Figure 5-4. Detail of the sleeve embroidery on the Afghani Nomad dress shown in Figure 5-1. Traditional and blue shisha mirrors were used and were surrounded by lazy daisies, chains, and French knots.

Figure 5-5. This design was created by Alexis Wright for a denim handbag.

Figure 5-6. Close-up of the stitches used on the denim handbag.

Figure 5-7. Further detail of the stitches used to fill the design shown in Figure 5-5. Cretan, outline, French knots and buttonhole stitches were the primary stitches used.

The design in Figure 5-5 was created for a denim handbag. The intricate stitching of the design is shown in Figure 5-6, and a further closeup is shown in Figure 5-7. Cretan stitches, French knots, outlines, buttonholes, and rope stitches, among others, were used. The designer used approximately two skeins each of D. M. C. embroidery floss in lavender, mauve, light gold, dark gold, light avocado, dark moss, and aqua. The mirrors were attached using Alexis Wright's method (see Figure 1-7) to further accentuate the symmetry of the design.

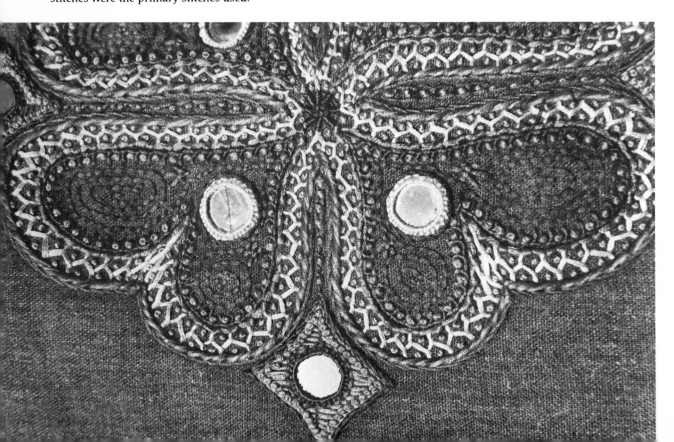

Figure 5-8. Alexis Wright had originally done this piece for a round pouch purse. She recycled the embroidery and put it onto a long patio dress.

Figure 5-9-A and -B. Pattern for the design shown in Figure 5-8 and detail of the stitches. The dotted line indicates the half mark of the design. The design can be used half or whole.

Another design made for a handbag is shown in Figure 5-8. The flower petal design was originally made for a pouch purse, but was later appliquéd onto a long patio skirt. The designer tired of her purse, but recycled her symmetrical design. Shades of red violet, green, gold, light blue, lavender, and dark gold were used for the stitching. She needed about two skeins of each of those colors in D.M.C. embroidery floss. Mirrors were first sewn on using Alexis Wright's method (see Figure 1-7). The embroidery stitches included the buttonhole, rope, spiderweb, lazy daisy, whipped chain, French knot, long-legged French knot, coral, woven fill, and crested chain. This design is particularly adaptable since it can be used in its round form or half of it can be used alone (see Figure 5-9-A and B). The intricate stitching used to fill in the design is shown in Figure 5-10.

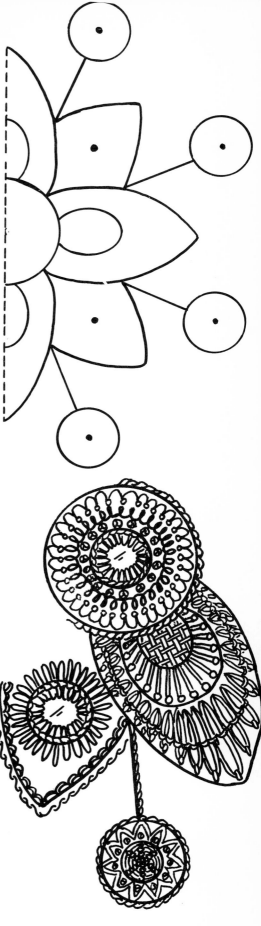

Figure 5-10. Detail view of the stitching used in the design shown in Figure 5-8. Whipped spiderwebs fill in the outer circles.

87

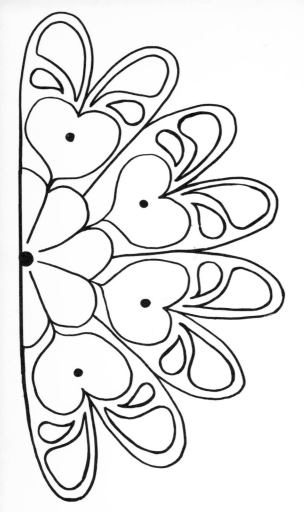

Figure 5-12. "Mandala" was filled in with intricate stitches and shisha mirrors and then the white linen piece was stretched over a wooden frame to be used as a wall hanging. Designed by Alexis Wright.

Figure 5-11-A and -B. Pattern for Alexis Wright's "Mandala" design and detail of stitches.

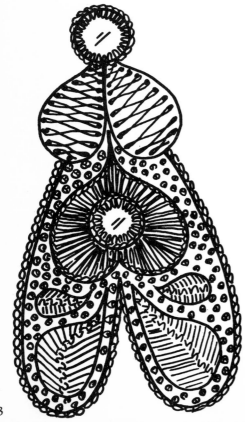

Another round, or half-round design is "Mandala," shown in Figure 5-11-A and -B, which was originally stitched for a wall hanging (see Figure 5-12). The design was worked on white linen and stretched over a wooden frame. Some of the stitches used were the chain, French knot, long-armed feather, closely worked buttonhole, rope (done in 12 strands of floss), outline, cretan, and van dyke (see Figure 5-11). Three skeins each of lavender, purple, deep green, old gold, wine red, yellow green, navy, blue with lavender tint, dark lavender, and moss embroidery floss were required.

The design shown in Figure 5-13 was worked on a piece of avocado green cotton fabric. When the embroidery was completed the design was cut out, leaving the fabric borders, and machine-zigzagged to the yoke of a cream-colored crushed muslin dress. A detail of the finished embroidery is shown in Figure 5-14. The mirrors were stitched on using Alexis Wright's method (see Figure 1-7) in rust-colored floss. Some of the other stitches used were the outline, spiderweb, cretan, French knot, coral, rope, and long-legged French knot. Two skeins each of aqua, old gold, rust, cinnamon, navy, and bittersweet orange were used.

The symmetrical design shown in Figure 5-15 was worked on burnt orange handwoven cotton. The embroidery was done using three skeins each of floss in aqua, deep avocado green, moss, mauve, rose pink, green, antique gold, old gold, lime, and bittersweet orange. A variety of stitches were used to achieve the textural relief. Needlewoven strips were done in old-gold floss. Some of the other stitches used were spiderwebs, French knots, chains, cretans, herringbones, outlines, ropes, corals, and Pekinese stitches.

Figure 5-13. Another design by Alexis Wright.

Figure 5-14. The design shown in *Figure 5-13* was filled with a variety of stitches, and when the embroidery was complete the piece was machine zigzagged to the yoke of a dress.

Figure 5-15. Rust-colored cotton was the background for this design. Spokes of needleweaving were used to achieve the three-dimensional effect. Designed by Alexis Wright.

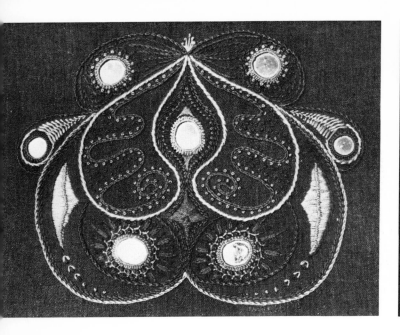

Figure 5-16. This design was worked for a fabric purse. Lots of French knots dot the outline stitching. Designed by Alexis Wright.

Figure 5-17. Vima Micheli made this design on the front of a denim tote bag. Her knotted detached buttonhole connects the five center mirrors, and needleweaving is done on the outer spokes surrounding the edge.

Figure 5-18. This wall hanging was made on vegetable-dyed fabric. Felt, sequins, shisha mirrors, and hishi beads are all part of the composition. Designed by Jill Henry.

Still another symmetrical design is shown in Figure 5-16. The French knots, outlines, cretans, lazy daisies, rope, buttonholes, and fishbones were worked onto blue denim in shades of gold, mauve, rose, moss, avocado green, and aqua D.M.C. floss.

Creative symmetrical designs are also shown in Figures 5-17 and 5-18. The design in 5-17 was originally made to embellish a denim tote. The five center mirrors were connected with the detached buttonhole stitch (see Figure 2-22) in D.M.C. pearl cotton, size #3, in bright lemon yellow. Surrounding the yellow detached buttonhole is a circle of more open, airy detached buttonholes in bright red D.M.C. pearl cotton size #3. The outer spokes are light green D.M.C. pearl cotton size #5, threads with occasional needleweaving over and under them done in dark green D.M.C. pearl cotton, size #3.

The design in Figure 5-18 was made for a wall hanging. The cotton fabric was hand-dyed using beets, which created the deep rose colored background. After attaching the center mirror, using Alexis Wright's method (see Figure 1-7), the spontaneous design was created working from the center outward. Sequins in iridescent black, felt strips in charcoal gray, black seed beads, and bits of abalone were used together in this unique design. The fabric was stretched over a wooden frame.

6

Mirrors with Needlepoint

Needlepoint has come a long way. Though preworked petit point floral canvases still exist, needlepoint has taken on new dimensions. Persian yarn in a kaleidoscope of colors, improved canvases, and various books giving a potpourri of textural stitches have contributed to a rebirth of this age-old art. Just as fabric can be decorated with mirrors, so can needlepoint canvas be adorned with mirrors. The effect you are trying to achieve determines whether or not you needlepoint the canvas before applying the mirror. Needlepoint can be beautiful by itself, but when mirrors, beads, floss, threads, and tassels are added, something magical happens. There are endless ways of using needlepoint—pillows and chair seats (of course!), pictures and purses, sandals and sashes, boleros and boxes, pincushions, and other paraphernalia. The sky and your imagination are the only limitations.

Materials
Needlepoint is a time-comsuming, but most relaxing and rewarding, craft. As I said in the Introduction, and I feel it bears repeating, time is a precious commodity. Therefore, since you are investing so much time, you might as well use the best-quality materials you can afford. It is pure fantasy to think that you can produce a first-rate piece with second-rate materials.

Canvas comes in many types—mono canvas (the easiest to work on), interlocking canvas (your work will retain its shape, but interlocking canvas tends to fray your yarn), and penelope canvas (which can also be used for petit point). Canvas comes in various mesh sizes. For example, 10/1 canvas means that there are ten holes per inch, or 100 holes per square inch; 12/1 canvas has twelve holes to the inch, or 144 holes in a square inch. With 12/1 canvas you generally have to split yarn and use only two strands; with 10/1 canvas you will use all three strands of Persian yarn. The more detail there is in a design, the smaller the canvas mesh you would use. My favorite size is 10/1, simply because I don't like to split strands of yarn. The designs in this chapter were designed to be worked on 10/1 mono canvas, also called #10 mono canvas.

There are many types of *yarn*. Persian yarns are widely available and come in a wide range of colors. Their luster and strength make them the ideal yarn to use for your needlepoint. Acrylics and blends may be less expensive than Persian yarns, but they are stretchy and are not as easy to work with. Persian carpets are all made with Persian yarns, so that should tell you something about their durability.

The best *needle* to use on 10/1 mono canvas is a #18 or a #20 tapestry needle. The point of a tapestry needle is blunt and will not split the threads of the canvas.

To prevent the edges of the canvas from fraying, apply *masking tape* along the edges before you begin your work. If you're feeling spiffy and happen to have a sewing machine, you can stitch on some double-fold seam binding instead.

Enlarging, Tracing, and Blocking

Follow the instructions for enlarging patterns on page 84. After you have your enlarged needlepoint pattern, you will need a waterproof marking pen to trace the pattern onto the canvas. This is very important because the canvas gets wet in the blocking process. There will be buckets of tears shed if, when your needlepoint gets wet, the ink runs all over your yarn. If you don't happen to have a professional light box (not many people do!), you can put a light under any glass table. Or, the next resort is a window—we all have those! Tape the design and the canvas to the window on a sunny day and trace.

Usually, needlepoint will require blocking after it has been completed. Blocking can be done by a professional blocker at a needlepoint finishers, at an upholsterers, or at a dry cleaner's. Also, the many books written on the subject of needlepoint provide detailed instructions on how to block needlepoint yourself. (See Barbara and Karl Guller's *Crewel Needlepoint World*, Van Nostrand Reinhold© 1973.)

Figure 6-1. Gwenn Stutzman combined a variety of needlepoint stitches with shisha mirrors to create a pillow entitled "Joy."

Designs

Now you are ready to begin stitching! The designs shown here are just some of the countless ideas possible with shisha mirrors on needlepoint. The pillow shown in Figure 6-1 and Color Plate 7, "Joy," is an example of the effect achieved by using a variety of textured stitches. Brick (done over four threads), gobelin, and diagonal tent stitches were used. The design would also be beautiful in continental stitch — a beginner's favorite. All of the needlepoint was completed and the piece was blocked before the mirrors were stitched on. The pattern for "Joy" is shown in Figure 6-2. If you want to make your own pillow, you will need about 2½ ounces of red, 1½ ounces of deep pink and dark orange, 1 ounce of light orange, and ½ ounce of magenta, gold, and medium orange Paternayan yarn. The design was done in brick stitch and gobelin stitch, while the background was done in diagonal tent stitch. The design should be done first, then the background, and then the mirrors should be attached with the cretan stitch method (see Figure 1-2).

Figure 6-2. Pattern for the Joy design shown in Figure 6-1.

Each square = 1"

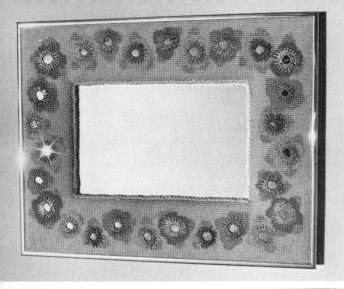

Figure 6-3. These mirrors surrounding a mirror are reminiscent of a Hawaiian lei. The diagonal tent stitch was used, and the shisha mirrors were stitched on with Glosilla thread by Bucilla. Designed by Gwenn Stutzman.

Figure 6-4. Pattern for the design shown in Figure 6-3.

Each square = 1"

Shisha mirrors are wonderful accents for needlepoint mirror frames. An Hawaiian-inspired design (see Figure 6-3 and Color Plate 8) was done in diagonal tent (sometimes called basketweave stitch) on 10/1 mono canvas. The diagonal tent stitch does not distort the canvas, so it is an ideal choice for this mirror frame. A lustrous six-strand thread was added to attach some of the mirrors, giving the piece a shiny look. Again, the needlepoint was completed before any of the shisha mirrors were added. Professional finishers added the large interior rope-twist edging and the rectangular mirror. The metal frame sets off the rectangular mirror, as well as the tiny shisha mirrors. The design for the mirror frame is shown in Figure 6-4. If you wish to duplicate the mirror frame, you will need about 2½ ounces of golden yellow Paternayan yarn and ½ ounce each in medium pink, light pink, light orange, medium orange, dark orange, and green. You will also need two skeins each of Glosilla® by Bucilla in magenta, orange, and golden yellow to stitch on the mirrors.

Pillows and needlepoint seem to go hand in hand. "Angels We Have Heard On High," shown in Figure 6-5 and Color

Plate 5, features an interesting use of mirrors. After the entire canvas was stitched, mirrors were added to the angel's hair. Then bullion stitches, made of single-strand Persian yarn, were added. The bullion stitch is shown in Figure 6-6. If you'd like to create an "Angels We Have Heard On High" pillow of your own, the pattern is shown in Figure 6-7. You will need 3¾ ounces of dark orange Paternayan yarn, 2 ounces of golden yellow, medium golden yellow, and light orange, ¾ ounce of plum, ½ ounce of pale pink, and ⅛ ounce of deep pink and magenta. For the tassels you will need a total of 12 ounces in medium golden yellow, light orange, medium orange, dark orange, and deep pink. The bullion stitches are done in ½ ounce of medium golden yellow. The body of the angel was done in diagonal tent stitches and then the French knots were added. The lettering and the border lines were done next, followed by the background, which was done in a brick stitch, covering four threads. After blocking, the bullion stitches were added. Tassels were done after the pillow had been assembled.

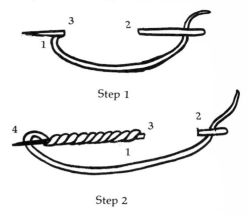

Figure 6-6. Making the bullion stitch.

Step 1

Step 2

Step 3

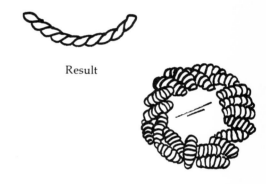

Result

Mirror with Bullion Stitches

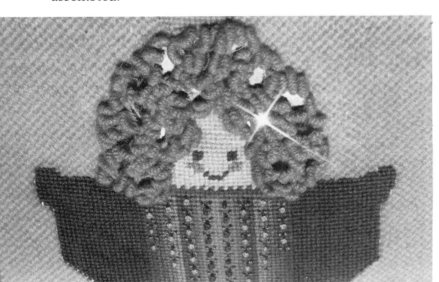

Figure 6-5. Detail of the angel on Gwenn Stutzman's pillow, "Angels We Have Heard On High." French knots of D. M. C. pearl cotton are the "roses" on the dress, and bullion stitches add to the lush look of the angel's hair.

Figure 6-7. Pattern for the design shown in Figure 6-5.

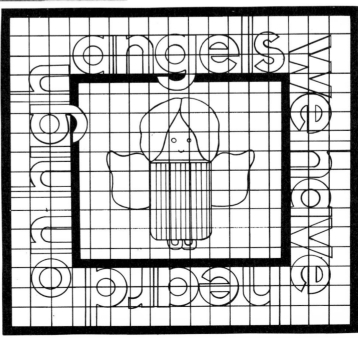

Notice the mirror eye in the needlepoint pillow entitled "Winking Sun" (see Figure 6-8 and Color Plate 11). (See *Lisbeth Perrone's Needlepoint Workbook*, by Lisbeth Perrone, Random House, © 1973.) For the body of the 10- by 10-inch pillow, which was done on #10 mono canvas, the designer used 1 ounce of Paternayan yarn in golden yellow and dark orange, ½ ounce in turquoise and ¼ ounce in plum, magenta, deep pink, medium pink, and moss. The mirrors were attached with Glosilla® by Bucilla in shades of orange and magenta. To add tassels you will need an additional ounce of yarn for each one.

Mirrors, as well as wooden beads and a variety of textured stitches, were added to the elephant design pillow, "Pillowphant," shown in Figure 6-9 and Color Plate 12. The body of the elephant was done in the diagonal tent stitch, using shading and blending techniques. The trapping on the elephant was done in bargello, and the pom-poms were cut turkey work. The 18- by 15-inch pillow was done on #12 mono canvas in Persian yarns in tones of gray, turquoise, moss green, plums, pinks, and oranges. After completing the needlepoint, the piece was blocked, the mirrors were attached, the beads were sewn on and the pillow was assembled. Lastly, a bright red tassel was added for the tail.

In addition to a multitude of other uses, needlepoint canvas can be made into bags and evening purses. The two evening bags shown in Figure 6-10 are beautiful examples of mirrors effectively combined with needlepoint. See Figure 6-11 for a closeup view. The designer used #12 mono needlepoint

Figure 6-8. "Winking Sun" is an adaptation of a Lisbeth Perrone's design, worked by Gwenn Stutzman. Basic needlepoint stitches, combined with dazzling colors and mirror embroidery, make this tassel-cornered pillow special.

Figure 6-9. Gwenn Stutzman adapted, stitched, and embellished this "Pillowphant" designed by DeDe Ogden for DeDe's Needleworks. Mirrors and beads add a touch of whimsy, and the tail is a fluffy tassel.

Figure 6-10. Petite needlepoint evening bags, accented with mirror embroidery, were made by Lucy Anderson. The handles are simply plastic bracelets from the dime store.

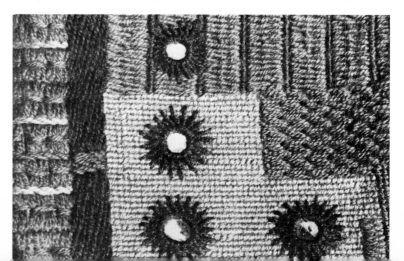

Figure 6-11. Detail of the needlepoint stitches used on the evening bags shown in Figure 6-10.

Figure 6-12. Mirrors and textural stitches were combined to create this exquisite needlepoint vest. The bird is the focal point of the vest back. Designed by Kay Whitcomb.

Figure 6-13. Detail of shisha mirrors and textural stitches on the back of the vest shown in Figure 6-12.

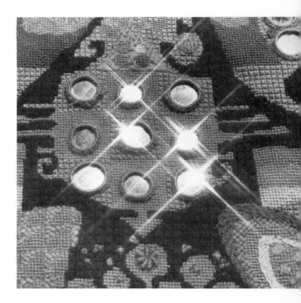

canvas, drew on geometric shapes using a waterproof marking pen, and proceeded to fill in the shapes with a variety of stitches. Some of these stitches were shell, knotted, fern, Oriental, chain, gobelin, Milanese, and the Byzantine. The work was done in shades of rust, cinnamon, mauve, purple, and wine. The mirrors were stitched on using the Lucy Anderson method (see Figure 1-4) and the bag was lined with purple silk. Lastly, the handles were added.

More examples of mirrors effectively combined with needlepoint are seen in Color Plates 9 and 10. "Moon" in Color Plate 9 was done in cool blues and greens, and the silver mirrors complement the silver threads. In Plate 10 the amber beads, gold metallic threads, and mirrors add spark to the sunny design.

Another example of the versatility of needlepoint is seen in the needlepointed vest shown in Figure 6-12. Textured stitches and mirrors combine to give an exotic feeling to this vest. To begin the project, the designer traced pieces from a commercial vest pattern onto #14 mono canvas. She then painted an original design onto the canvas using acrylic paints. The mirrors were added and the needlepoint stitching began. For the vest, chain, cross, Scotch, gobelin, brick, and diagonal tent stitches were used, along with French knots and spiderweb stitches. Persian yarns in shades of American beauty red, dark royal blue, scarlet, orange, dark rose, mauve, ochre, charcoal, and light gray were chosen for this dramatic piece. A detail of the bird on the back of the vest is shown in Color Plate 20. Both amber and silver shisha mirrors were used. Figure 6-13 shows an extreme closeup of the mirrors on the bird. On the front of the vest the designer combined decorative stitches with a cluster of mirrors (see Figure 6-14). The mirrors were attached directly onto unworked needlepoint canvas to give a "sunken in" feeling. A soft ring of Persian yarn, in a size slightly smaller than the shisha mirror, was made by wrapping the yarn around a finger and doing the buttonhole stitch over the yarn wrapping. (See Figure 3-22 showing the buttonhole stitch over a "hard" ring made of plastic.) The soft ring was then placed on top of the shisha mirror and tacked here and there to hold the ring and the shisha mirror underneath onto the needlepoint canvas.

Figure 6-14. Detail of another area on the needlepoint vest shown in Figure 6-12.

7

Delightful Mirrored Dolls

Figure 7-1. Barbara Chapman transformed a yellow stocking into this delightful doll. Antique mirrored cloth is used for the dress, and cord was wrapped and coiled for the wings. Wire was covered and twisted into a crazy hairdo.

Dolls can soothe a scraped knee, lull us to sleep at night, be our best friend, and be a guest at tea parties. Childhood memories linger, and many of us, including myself, have a special place in our hearts for dolls. In many ways we remain children in grown-up bodies. Making and decorating dolls is one "socially acceptable" way to turn back the hands of time. Handmade dolls can be given as a gift to show our love for someone special, or they can be kept in our homes merely to enjoy. Dolls come in many varieties — china, plastic, rubber, stuffed, crying, wetting, and Barbie. But the dolls in this chapter all have one thing in common. They have all been embellished with mirrors.

The charming doll shown in Figure 7-1 was made by a designer who uses intense colors and whose eclectic use of materials and techniques give her dolls a special look. Mirrors fit in perfectly. It's hard to believe, but the base of this doll is a yellow cotton stocking! Antique mirror cloth makes the dress, and the wings were coiled by wrapping wool yarn over jute in the American Indian basket technique. The hair is wrapped wire that has been twisted into a zany hairdo. Jingle jangles hang from the curls and make a joyful sound when the doll is picked up to be cuddled. The angel in Figure 7-2 is another delightful creation. The shisha mirrors were sewn on with metallic thread.

Little Mr. Wise Owl would make just about any child smile (see Figure 7-3) and shisha mirrors are perfect for his eyes. The owl is made from felt — dandy to work with because it does not ravel and can even be glued. Feather, buttonhole, and cretan stitches were used on the orange and yellow felt.

A more sophisticated use of mirrors is seen in Figure 7-4. Sequins, velvet, and metallic threads are an important part of "Madonna and Child." "Victorian Doll" (see Figure 7-5) is made of chocolate-brown velvet and has handspun hair. Note the intricate stitching of mirrors down the front of the doll's dress. The stitching is done in gold metallic thread. Further examples of superbly decorated and constructed dolls are seen in Color Plates 25, 26, 27, 28, 29, 30, and 32. Note the bold colors, ethnic fabrics, and the use of interesting trinkets.

Figure 7-3. Felt appliquèd onto felt is the background for this simple owl. Shisha mirrors are the stars in the eyes! The owl is used as a doorstop in the author's home and was a gift from Jeannie Anderson.

Figure 7-2. This whimsical angel was made with bits and pieces of fabric that had been festooned with shisha mirrors. The halo is slightly askew! Designed by Barbara Chapman.

Figure 7-4. The Mexican "Santos" inspired Maureen Flores to make this soft sculpture "Madonna and Child" from chocolate brown velvet, shiny sequins, and sparkling shisha mirrors.

Figure 7-5. Handspun yarn for hair, gold lamè thread, a lace skirt, and shisha mirrors all combine on the velvet body of this Victorian doll. Designed by Maureen Flores.

Suppliers

Lucy Anderson
Box 1192
Palos Verdes Estates, CA 90274
Lucy Anderson makes custom-made dresses adorned with shisha mirrors.

Bazaar Del Mundo
2754 Calhoun St.
San Diego, CA 92110
Diane Powers runs this complex of shops in "Old Town" in San Diego. Put it at the top of your "Must See List." There are ethnic fabrics, yarns, threads, and other fantastic goodies. If it can't be purchased here, it means the item is probably not available anywhere! Classes are taught in shisha mirror embroidery, tassel making, needlepoint, and more.

Berger Specialty Co.
413 East 8th St.
Los Angeles, CA 90014
Available are wood beads, metal beads, shinies, and lots of other jewelry findings. You may order through the mail.

Boutique Margot
26 West 54th St.
New York City, NY 10019
Margot carries a complete line of D.M.C. threads. You may order through the mail.

Bucilla
30-20 Thomson Ave.
Long Island City, NY 11101
Write to them to find the nearest supplier of Glosilla thread (six-strand rayon embroidery floss in a rainbow of colors).

D.M.C.
107 Trumbull St.
Elizabeth, NJ 07206
Available through the mail are threads, floss, and pearl cotton.

DeDe's Needleworks — Designs by DeDe Ogden
3990 Washington St.
San Francisco, CA 94118
DeDe Ogden does manificent needlepoint designs, including the elephant design, "Pillowphant" on page 96.

Design Research
53 East 57th St.
New York, NY 10022
Marimekko fabrics are sold here. Design Research has branches in Beverly Hills, San Francisco, and Cambridge, as well as other major cities.

Elpa Marketing Industries
Atlantic and Thorens Ave.
New Hyde Park, NY 11040
Swiss music boxes are available through the mail.

Eye of the Needle
Vintage 1870
Yountville, CA 94599
Vintage 1870 is a group of quaint shops located in the old Grozinger Winery. At Eye of the Needle they sell fabrics and yarns and feature classes in shisha mirrors, needlepoint, etc. They also carry D.M.C. threads.

Folkloric Yarns
522 Ramona St.
Palo Alto, CA 94302
Available are high luster yarns, gold and silver threads from Spain, Mexican floss, and other unique threads and yarns.

Folkwear Patterns
Box 98
Forestville, CA 95436
Ethnic dress and blouse patterns are available here. You may order through the mail.

Handcrafts From Europe
Box 372
Sausalito, CA 94965
Floor-to-ceiling trimmings fill this quaint shop overlooking San Francisco Bay. They also have a complete line of D.M.C. threads and Paternayan yarns.

Idle Hands
82-04 Medford Blvd.
Kew Gardens, NY 11415
Metallic threads in copper, gold, silver, blue, and red. You may order through the mail.

It's A Stitch
4446½ Forman Ave.
Toluca Lake, CA 91602
A cute shop with a complete line of needlepoint supplies, Paternayan yarns, and D.M.C. threads. You may order through the mail. Classes are taught in shisha mirror embroidery, tassel making, and needlepoint.

Kitsophrenia, Inc.
Box 5042
Glendale, CA 91201
Shisha mirrors, pom-poms, jingle jangles, and shinies from Pakistan and India are available through mail order only. Send a self-addressed stamped envelope for a brochure. They also carry tin-framed mirrors and "dancing bells."

Needlecraft Shop
4501 Van Nuys Blvd.
Sherman Oaks, CA 91403
D.M.C. threads, Paternayan yarns, and quality needlepoint supplies are available. You may also order through the mail. Purple hectograph pencils are available.

Paternayan Yarns
312 E. 95th St.
New York, NY 10028
Write to Paternayan for a supply source near you.

Rusty Needle
1140 Coast Highway
Laguna Beach, CA 92651
A charming shop where classes are taught in ethnic clothing construction, tassel making, needlepoint, and various other subjects.

Jean Simpson
1614 Ard Eevin Ave.
Glendale, CA 91202
I am a lecturer and teacher of shisha mirror embroidery and tassel making.

Gwenn Stutzman
#1 Winged Foot Dr.
Novato, CA 94547
Gwenn custom creates needlepoint designs and painted canvases. She also teaches needlepoint.

Vima, s.p.a.
2727 Marconi Ave.
Sacramento, CA 95821
Vima Micheli owns this special shop. D.M.C. threads, yarns, and many unique items are available. There are classes in shisha mirror embroidery, tassel making, needlepoint, stitchery, and other subjects.

Kay Whitcomb
Box 721
La Jolla, CA 92038
Kay designs custom needlepoint and sells her canvases.

Alexis Wright
42 Quarterdeck
Pacific Grove, CA 93950
Alexis custom-makes shisha mirror hangings, purses, etc. She is also a teacher of embroidery and mirror work.

Index